University of London Classical Studies

II

THE HALIEUTICA
ASCRIBED TO OVID

The
HALIEUTICA
ascribed to Ovid

EDITED BY
J. A. RICHMOND

UNIVERSITY OF LONDON
THE ATHLONE PRESS
1962

Published by
THE ATHLONE PRESS
UNIVERSITY OF LONDON
at 2 Gower Street, London WC1
Distributed by Constable & Co. Ltd
12 *Orange Street, London* WC2

Canada
University of Toronto Press

U.S.A.
Oxford University Press Inc.
New York

Printed in Great Britain by
WILLIAM CLOWES AND SONS LIMITED
London and Beccles

FOREWORD

This edition of the *Halieutica* has been condensed from portions of the Ph.D. thesis I submitted to the University of London in 1957. It contains the materials on which any discussion of the authorship must be based, and, although I believe Ovid was not the author, I have tried to preserve an open mind while preparing my text. Few indeed will read the *Halieutica* for its literary excellence, since it has practically none, but the short poem is a not unimportant one for scholars. This book is published to provide them with a detailed critical and philological discussion of the many problems in which it abounds. The metrical difficulties, however, and the tangled question of the sources are problems the solution of which must depend on the text as established by the use of internal evidence, and such external evidence as does not involve the assumption of the author's identity. These problems require a lengthy treatment, which would spoil the proportion of this book if they were included. Furthermore they are special problems that must interest only a fraction of the many readers who may have occasion to refer to the *Halieutica*. Hence I have reserved them for discussion elsewhere. There are several excellent modern works on classical ichthyology, and consequently I have refrained from burdening my commentary with information which may readily be obtained from them.

I could never have undertaken the preparation of this work had I not been awarded a post-graduate studentship by the University of London, and I am glad to have this opportunity of expressing my appreciation. It is fitting that I should also indicate my obligations to the kindness and help of the following scholars. Professor O. Skutsch, of University College London, suggested the subject, guided my research, helped me in innumerable matters of detail, criticized the work at every stage, and has left me indebted to him, both as a friend and a scholar, to a degree that makes not only repayment but even

acknowledgment quite impossible. Professor Eric G. Turner of
the Institute of Classical Studies (London), who had already
shown me very great personal kindness, gave special assistance
in arranging for publication. Mr. E. J. Kenney, of Peterhouse,
Cambridge, who examined my thesis, contributed many
valuable suggestions. Professor R. Keydell of Berlin sent me
several letters containing his comments on, and criticism of,
theories I advanced. Mr. Eric W. Handley, of University
College London, gave me considerable help on questions of
palaeography.

Photographs of the Mss. were supplied to me by the *Öster-
reichische Nationalbibliothek* and the *Institut de Recherche et
d'Histoire des Textes*. The Librarians and staff of the following
institutions did everything possible to help me: The British
Museum, The Bodleian Library, The Institute of Classical
Studies (London), Trinity College, Dublin, The National
Library of Ireland, The University Libraries of Göttingen,
Bonn, and Cologne, University College London, University
College, Dublin.

When seeking information on fishing or zoology, or looking
for help with typewriting or proof-reading, I have never
called in vain on the patience of my personal friends.

J. A. R.

CONTENTS

ABBREVIATIONS

MODERN WORKS are cited by using the author's name only, if the reference is to a work listed in the *Index Bibliographicus* on p. 113 *et sq.* A key word from the title is added if necessary.

ANCIENT AUTHORS are cited generally in accordance with the practice of the *Thesaurus Linguae Latinae* and Liddell-Scott-Jones' *Greek Lexicon*.

For PERIODICALS the conventions established by J. Marouzeau in *L'Année Philologique* have been used.

SPECIAL ABBREVIATIONS

Aelian	Aelian: *De Natura Animalium*
Aristotle *or* Ar.	Aristotle's works on Natural History, viz.:
	pp. 486–638: *Historia Animalium*
	pp. 639–697: *De Partibus Animalium*
	pp. 698–704: *De Motu Animalium*
	pp. 704–714: *De Incessu Animalium*
	pp. 715–789: *De Generatione Animalium*
Atti	My article in *Atti del Convegno Internazionale Ovidiano*
Birt	T. Birt, *De Halieuticis Ovidio poetae falso adscriptis*
CLA	E. A. Lowe, *Codices Latini Antiquiores*
CMG	*Corpus Medicorum Graecorum* (Leipzig, 1908 –)
DT	D'A. W. Thompson, *A Glossary of Greek Fishes* (the figures that follow are page references)
Forcellini	A. Forcellini and V. de-Vit, *Totius Latinitatis Lexicon* (Prato, 1858–79)
N.L.	W. M. Lindsay, *Notae Latinae*
Oppian *or* Opp.	Oppian, *Halieutica*
Pliny *or* Plin.	Pliny the Elder, *Naturalis Historia*
PLM	*Poetae Latini Minores* (various editions)

Plutarch	Plutarch, *De Sollertia Animalium*
RE	Pauly-Wissowa, *Realencyclopädie der classischen Altertumswissenschaft* (Stuttgart, 1894 –)
Schenkl	H. Schenkl, 'Zur Kritik . . . des Grattius und anderer lateinischer Dichter'
SVF	J. von Arnim, *Stoicorum Veterum Fragmenta* (Leipzig, 1903–24)
ThLL	*Thesaurus Linguae Latinae* (Leipzig, 1900 –)

Ovid is usually cited in accordance with the practice of *A Concordance to Ovid*, by R. J. Deferrari and others (Washington, 1939), viz.:

A	*Amores*
AA	*Ars Amatoria*
Ep.	*Epistulae Heroidum*
EP	*Epistulae ex Ponto*
F	*Fasti*
M	*Metamorphoses*
MF	*De Medicamine Faciei Femineae*
RA	*Remedia Amoris*
T	*Tristia*

PROLEGOMENA

I. PALAEOGRAPHIC

A. Codex Vindobonensis 277

Jacopo Sannazaro (*aliter* 'Sannazzaro'), or, to give him his latinized name, Actius Syncerus,[1] the distinguished Renaissance poet and scholar, in the year 1502, or thereabouts,[2] discovered in Central France a classical manuscript which contained the following works:

'Versus Eucheriae poetrie',[3] vv. 21–32	(55 r.)
'Versus Ouidi de piscibus et feris'	(55 r.–58 r.)
An elegiac couplet[4] 'Ceruus aper . . .'	(58 r.)
'Gratti Cynegeticon Lib. I'	(58 v.–70 v.)
Select epigrams from Martial (written by a different hand)	(71 r.–73 v.)

These sheets are bound in *Codex Vindobonensis 277*, and the figures in brackets are the folio numbers of the codex. Haupt has given the symbol A to these sheets (quires 17 and 18 of an ancient codex[5]). The second item in the list consists of 130 lines of hexameter verse which have been identified as the work quoted by Pliny the Elder, in the thirty-second book of his *Natural History*, under the description [*uolumen*] *quod Halieuticon inscribitur* (Pliny 32.11; cf. 32.152).

The writing of the Ms. is pre-Caroline minuscule.[6] There is, in general, restraint and simplicity in the handwriting, and the wilder forms of Merovingian hand (e.g. the sloped shaft of *h*) do not appear. Nevertheless, the grace and formality of the

---

[1] There is a good article on Sannazaro (s.v.) in the *Enciclopedia Italiana*.

[2] For details see the preface to Haupt's edition (Leipzig, 1838), p. xxii; R. Sabbadini, *Le scoperte dei codici latini e greci* (Florence, 1905), p. 165.

[3] *Anth. Lat.* 390.   [4] *Anth. Lat.* 391.   [5] Cf. Schenkl, p. 399.

[6] Apograph and good commentary in Schenkl, pp. 387 *et sq.* The preface to Vollmer's edition (*Poetae latini minores*, 2.i (Leipzig, 1911)) is also good.

Caroline hand have not been achieved, and there remain many
features of Merovingian origin. In *general* character the hand
may be compared with that of 'Cologne, Dombibliothek 76,
folio 185 r.',[1] and that of *Paris. lat. 1839*.[2] For our purposes it is
safest to date the Ms. in a tentative manner at *saec. viii ex.*, or
perhaps even *saec. ix in.* E. Chatelain, in his *Paléographie des
classiques latins* (Paris, 1884–92), in pl. 101, reproduces folios
55 v. and 56 r. (vv. 10–52). I have examined photographs of the
Ms. and compared them with the apograph given by H.
Schenkl.

Vollmer in his introduction[3] has a list of errors that occur in
Schenkl's apograph. I note a few errors that Vollmer did not
detect. *V. 39:* the Ms. here has *conticitatus*. The *ti* (taken as *ci* by
Schenkl) is written with a ligature, and a dot has been placed
on either side. Schenkl, followed by Vollmer and Lenz, has
been misled by the badly-formed lower loop of the *t*, which
seems to form a straight line with the right-hand dot, and gives
the impression of a stroke made to cancel the letters. No such
ligature as that assumed for *ci* has come to my notice. *V. 95:*
for the Ms. *tergor&*, Schenkl, Vollmer, and Lenz report
tergore &. *V. 116:* the Ms. has *I&* corrected to *Ict*. Schenkl
takes the dot under the *&* as a subscript *u*. He is followed by
Vollmer and Lenz. One or two doubtful points are noticed in
the apparatus.

'Interpunktion kennt die Handschrift nicht', claims Schenkl,
p. 415. There seem to me to be some traces of punctuation.
Stops, more or less clear, may be seen at the ends of vv. 1, 6, 8,
9, 22, 24, 30, 93, 105; and there is punctuation in the line at
vv. 90 (*Num uada subnatis. Imo uiridentur. ab herbis*), 94 (*Nam
gaudent pelago. quales. scombrique bouesque*), and 103 (*Cantharus
ingratus suco. tum. concolor illi*). These stops seem to mark logical
pauses. *Quidni*, v. 59, has what seems like a macron over the
last two letters. I am indebted to Mr. E. J. Kenney for the
explanation of this curious feature which puzzled me for a long
time. The scribe read *Quid nisi* as *Qui dni si* and, taking *dni* as
domini, superimposed the dash which was used to indicate the
nomina sacra.

---

[1] Reproduced in Jones, pl. iv (2) (dated *saec. viii*), p. 30.
[2] *CLA* 5.701—second hand (dated *saec. viii ex.*).   [3] P. 5 (adn. (2)).

I shall not here give a detailed description of the Ms. There are a few points of interest, however, to which I should like to refer.

B. *Severe damage to text*

The reader cannot but be impressed by the damaged state of the text. Several lacunae exist which cannot be doubted, and in this edition more will be suggested. The probability of some transpositions has also to be considered. Although I cannot suggest any comprehensive theory that would account for the great injuries the text has suffered, and indeed I believe that the damage may have occurred in two or more stages, I think I should refer to the more remarkable features, which show that an ancestor of our Ms. was mutilated. Thus v. 10, *Sin . . .*, pretty clearly lay at the foot of a *recto* page, and all the verse was lost save for the first syllable. Colour is lent to this hypothesis by the corresponding fragment of v. 25, which would seem to have been at the end of a line on the *verso* side of the same folio. This gap would indicate a page of 15 verses, and Schenkl,[1] following an attempt by Birt,[2] tries to reconstruct an ancestor manuscript's pagination. Schenkl assumes a page varying between 13 and 15 lines which rather convincingly agrees with the gap of 13 lines between the two occurrences of v. 52 (65a). He then finds that v. 134 would end a page of his hypothetical Ms., and that Grattius shows evidence of having continued the book with 14 verses to a page. His figures are plausible, yet not quite convincing, for the following reasons:

(*a*) He has to assume pages with varying numbers of lines; this deprives the demonstration of desirable rigour.

(*b*) He relies on the loss of a *whole* line at Grattius, v. 59, as evidence for the loss of a line at the foot of a page, yet the fragment at *Halieutica*, v. 127, and the gap after *concolori*, v. 124, which are also evidence for the foot of a page, are not brought into account.

(*c*) No account of the lacunae between vv. 81 and 91 is given.

[1] P. 417 *et sq.* ('ich habe aber . . . die ganze Frage fallen gelassen . . .').
[2] P. 104.

Although I must agree with Schenkl that his case is not demonstrated, yet I am attracted by the hypothetical page of 13–15 lines, as it would provide some slight support for the lacuna I place after v. 101, since the gap at 127–9 is in just the corresponding position of the page 28 lines—i.e. 2 pages—further on. I believe, however, that the loss of several lines between vv. 81 and 91 makes it impossible convincingly to reconstruct the ancestor manuscript's pagination.[1]

c. *Is* Vindob. 277 *derived from Beneventum?*

I caution the reader against accepting the suggestion Lenz makes (p. 8) that the Ms. has been copied from a Beneventan exemplar. His ground for this belief is the confusion of *a* and *at* that he characterizes as Beneventan. And so indeed it is, but Lenz fails to explain why it occurs only in the diphthong *ae*.[2] The explanation was given by Schenkl: minuscule ligatured *ae* was misread as *ate*. It was at this time that the Beneventan hand was just being developed,[3] and the meagre evidence Lenz adduces is insufficient.

The indications of insular influence, which rather tell against Lenz's suggestion, are worth summarizing:

(*a*) Orthography: confusion of double *s*—*submisus* (24); hesitation on *quassat* (41); *emiso* (62); *generosso* (73) (cf. *CLA* 2 *passim*—but some of the cases may be explained as the result of French influence—cf. Havet, § 1079, on *Hal.* 24).

(*b*) Confusion of the *cum* and *con* symbols—*cumcursisque* (6). The insular symbol for *cum* is identical with the continental symbol for *con* (*N.L.* 41, 324).

---

[1] The page of 14 lines, or so, is not so improbable as Schenkl claims. Cf. Clark, p. 45.

[2] *a* is often read as *at* (cf. *dammate*, v. 4, and other examples in vv. 70, 71, 91, 110, 112, 113, 114, 120, 124, (126)). The repeated verse (52=65a) shows two stages of the corruption. In v. 52 (*irter*) we seem to have, in the letter like *t*, a careful but ignorant copy of a form of *a* (resembling the double *c* form on its side) commonly used in ligature in pre-Caroline and early minuscule. It can be seen how the scribe would take the form in v. 52 as a *t* preceded by a suprascript *a* (suprascript *a* was a common feature of the Merovingian script: Rand, p. 57). Thus verse 65a shows *irate*, which is the development we have seen in other cases. Cf. Schenkl, p. 421.

[3] Cf. Lowe, *The Beneventan Script*, p. 122, where the 'tentative period' is dated to '*saec. viii ex.—ix ex.*'.

(*c*) Confusion of the *in* and *inter* symbols—*In* for *inter* (85) (*N.L.* 113, and especially 111).

(*d*) The use of the predominantly insular symbol 7 for *et* in v. 107, where it would seem that our scribe was pressed for space and used this unobtrusive symbol.

(*e*) Confusion of *n*, *r*, *s* (doubtful)—? *uimens sub* (13); *sanguiṣne* (123); ? *more⟨na⟩ ferox*[1] (27); *mestes* (51) (cf. Lindsay, *Introduction*, p. 88).

It may be noted that points (*c*) and (*e*) indicate that insular writing lay in a text copied by a continental scribe, but that the other points seem to be peculiarities of an insular scribe. The use of the ligature for *nt* in mid-word—*mentis*, v. 59—suggests German influence (cf. e.g. *CLA* 1.108).

D. *Frequent simple palaeographic errors*

The following errors frequently occur, and examples are given here for facility of reference:

> confusion of *a* and *e*: e.g. *demmae*, v. 64.
> confusion of *a* and *u*: e.g. *mulas*, v. 123.
> confusion of *c* and *e*: e.g. *pietate*, v. 110.

E. *Comparison of the textual tradition in Grattius and the* Halieutica

The evidence points to a great difference in textual history between the *Cynegetica* of Grattius and our *Halieutica*. Cf. Schenkl, p. 420 *et sq.*

(*a*) We may note that the *Cynegetica* has no errors like *cateso* (v. 71) where *ae* has become *ate*. As remarked, the *Halieutica* shows some dozen cases (v. p. 4, *sup.*).

(*b*) The lines in the *Halieutica* begin, as a rule, with majuscules; those in Grattius with minuscules.

(*c*) The abbreviated form of *que*, with *q* followed by a mark like *s*, is to be found frequently in the *Halieutica* but does not occur in the *Cynegetica*.

(*d*) There are certain errors in Grattius which suggest a version in capitals or uncials (e.g. *sanoycae* for *sandyce* (86); *grudia* for *gaudia* (207); *claucum* for *glaucum* (503)).[2] I have not been able to find any corresponding errors in the *Halieutica*.

---

[1] In our text *a* is often read as *e*—*demmae* (64), *ruminet* (119), etc.
[2] So Schenkl, p. 420.

2—H.

Hence we cannot safely apply the palaeographic conclusions
to be drawn from Grattius to the criticism of our text.

F. *Relationship with* Paris. lat. 8071

There is a second (presumably French) Ms. (named B by
Haupt), *Paris. lat. 8071*,[1] that contains the matter found in
those sheets of *Vindob. 277* which we have just considered. In
1896 Traube, in his review of Postgate's *Corpus* (vol. 1),
remarked: 'Die ursprüngliche Vermutung Haupts, die er im
Besitze nicht hinlänglich genauer Kollationen wieder auf-
geben musste, das nämlich der Thuaneus[2] (*Paris lat. 8071*) eine
Abschrift des Sannazarianus (*Wien 277*) sei, bestätigt sich
jetzt vollkommen für jeden, der das Bild des letzteren bei
Chatelain (*Paléographie d. classiques latins*, pl. 101) mit Haupts
Apparat vergleicht' (*BPhW* 16 (1896), col. 1050). This judgment was confirmed by Schenkl (note especially his reconstruction of A and B, p. 400) in 1898, and Vollmer in 1911
(p. 7); and Owen (p. x) curiously remarks '. . . post insignes
Traubi curas, qui Parisinum ex Vindobonensi fluxisse
ostendit . . .'

In 1925 Heraeus, in the introduction (p. iv) to his edition of
Martial, refers to the opinion of Traube, and adds 'est tamen
quod dubites'. Lenz, in his edition, stresses these doubts, and
receives the readings of B into his apparatus. Lenz admits
(p. 12) that in support of Traube, 'stant tot, tam arti, tamque
fidi consensus exempla, ut refragantem recentioremque
codicem apographon esse negantem paene irrideas . . .', but
goes on to mention errors that he does not think could have
arisen from A. Owen had already claimed that B showed the
truth in *scurpius* (5), *emisso* (62), and *elops* (96). In the latter
case the reading of A is to be preferred (see notes *infra* on
v. 96), and, as Lenz remarks, in the other two cases no great
skill at emendation is required to correct the obvious errors.

[1] The script is Caroline minuscule of the ninth (or early tenth?) century. The
Ms. is described by C. Clementi, *Pervigilium Veneris*[3] (Oxford, 1936), p. 39 *et sq.*;
and on p. 172 *et sq.* there are photographs of the script. Cf. Schenkl, p. 399 *et sq.*,
for some ingenious reconstruction of the history of this Ms.

[2] So called because once the property of de Thou.

Lenz does not set out the errors in B that point clearly to A as a source.

Very significant[1] are places where the scribe of A made an error and corrected it in the succeeding letter. These instances show that the correct reading was before the scribe of A and that the blunder was made, and corrected, by him. Thus in v. 39 the scribe of A read *conci* in his exemplar, but inadvertently wrote *conti*, which he corrected to *conṭici*, which the scribe of B took (or corrected) as *contrici*.[2] A glance at Chatelain, as Traube remarks, will confirm the force of this argument. Similarly, in v. 123, *sanguine* lay before scribe A, but he wrote *sanguis*, and corrected to *sanguiṣne*, which scribe B wrote as *sanguis ne*. In *morsu* (version before A), written *uersu* (v. 44), corrected *u̇ẹrsu*, written by B as *mouersu*, the same phenomenon is to be seen. I set out the main variants in B that show it was copied from a text with the casual peculiarities we find in A: *mundum* (3), *teneracoiam* (3), *sicesʂarus* (9), *stillit* (35), *iacet* (116), *limas egat* (48) (details in Haupt's apparatus).

texse (107) is an interesting case. From the reading in A it is fairly clear that the scribe was pressed for space towards the end of the line. He accordingly decided to use the contraction 7 for *et*. The symbol 7 is not found elsewhere in A, so we may assume that the scribe here introduced the form. Now it is evident from the reading in B that scribe B found a symbol that he read as '*t*'. Since this can hardly be anything other than our 7, we can infer that A was the copy from which B was derived. (It is perhaps worth remark that where B has *rzer* (52) (so Haupt), *czeroleaque* (104), and *demme* (64), the errors can be explained by reference to the form of *a* that occurs in these cases in A.) In my opinion these cases furnish reasonably conclusive proof that the A is either an immediate or a more remote ancestor of B.

Before proceeding to examine Lenz's objections it may be useful to provide a list of passages where the scribe of B would seem to have set out to correct A. I asterisk the conjectures that seem to be justified: *scurpius** (5); *escam* (11); *obcurrere* (12)*;

---

[1] Cf. Lindsay, *Introduction*, p. 65: 'Mistakes of this kind are usually the best evidence of the derivation of one MS from another.'

[2] How *ti* resembles *tr* may be seen from Rand, pl. A (No. 24).

*uimen sub** (13); *caude** (13); *in equor** (14); *escarum* (16); *atq: ita*
(17); *ridet* (24); *connexat* (28); *contigit* (34); *amos* (i.e. *hamos*)
(45); *Quodque* (55); *emisso** (62). It will be noted that the quality
of the criticism seems to have deteriorated quickly as the scribe
progressed.

Lenz, having noted that the scribe attempts to correct the
text, claims that the alterations are such as show the scribe of B
to be 'non imprudentem'. How then, he asks, could he have
written wild variants that find no authority in A?[1]; and he lists
the following variants as probably being derived from an ancestor common to A and B (Lenz, pp. 12–13).

Index	Reading of A	Reading of B	Verse
(a)	sic manuq; minatur	quæ manuque miratur	2
(b)	dampro natareto	dam pronata retro (?—reto *lego*)	15
(c)	mouet quae	uomet que	47
(d)	demmae	demeæ	64
(e)	Vinculas abspoliis	Vinculas abs polus	74
(f)	echena ir	et hena ir	99
(g)	synodantes	sino dantes (*sic* B) (dentes L.)	107
(h)	rante	rantte	126
(i)	Sin *in text*	Sin *in margin*	10
(j)	in auras *ends line*	in auras *begins line*	25
(k)	redet	ridet	24
(l)	connextat	connexat	28
(m)	interuienit	interuiennit	30
(n)	coci	quoci (*pr. man.*)	85
(o)	pomphile	phomphi	101

So far from making Lenz's point, the cases (d), (l) (as just
remarked), and (c) (what Havet (§ 470) terms 'Anasyllabisme';
cf. Housman, *JPh* 18 (1890), p. 14, *et alibi*) seem merely to
argue against him. Case (n) seems to echo the French pronunciation of *q* and has been corrected. Cases (e), (f), and (m) seem
to reflect the script of A. Cases (i), (j), and (k) show the correct-
ing tendency of scribe B. Cases (a) and (b) were already
heavily corrupted and the scribe met them early in the poem
when his critical powers were not yet exhausted; in case (a)
one may alternatively compare the intrusion of *que* in *effugitq:*
and *insequiturq:* (80, 81), and conclude that sheer carelessness
has been the cause of the variant. I think that if one is to

---

[1] It is not impossible that a first copy of A had the corrections, and that a scribe
working from the copy introduced many of the further errors in B.

attribute any weight to the remaining cases ((g), (h), and (o)), one will be hard put to explain any minor blunders on the part of a copyist.

I trust that the reader now agrees that the indications of any independence in B are so shadowy that, in the face of the concrete evidence on the other side, one must concur with the eminent Traube and his successors. Hence, I have based my apparatus on A alone, save where I quote what I believe are the correct conjectures of B.

G. *Miscellaneous*

For completeness it is worth noting the other Ms. versions of the poem. Sannazaro (but cf. Schenkl, p. 392) made two copies, one of which is bound in *Vindob. 277* with A,[1] and the other is to be found in *Vindob. 3261*.[2] A further copy is to be found in the Milanese *Codex Ambros. S 81 sup.*[3] (There is an apograph by G. Galbiati of the latter in *Raccolta di scritti in onore di Felice Ramorino*, Milan (?1927), pp. 576–9.) The readings of all three are given by Schenkl in his apparatus. It would seem that the Ambrosian codex was the work of a scholar who desired to reconcile the text with Pliny by changing the title to *Halieuticon* and omitting the passage 49–91. Sannazaro's work is worthy of the opportunity he had as the first scholar to tackle the text, and he has obviously read Pliny with care, and applied sound judgment to the text. Allowance must be made for the difficulties under which Sannazaro worked—bad texts, and the lack of the aids that lie at the modern scholar's hand.

As a curiosity one may note here the forged *Halieutica* which Sertorius Quadrimanus sent to Columna, and which is printed by Columna in his edition (Naples, 1590) of Ennius (p. 246 *et sq.*). This poem has been concocted from portions of our text, and, although Haupt (p. xxvi) is inclined to believe that Quadrimanus acted in good faith, we read in the *Enciclopedia Italiana* (s.v. Quattromani, Sertorio), 'come critico, il Quattromani si divertì a punzecchiare gli umanisti, enumerando i debiti che il Petrarcha aveva con la poesia provenzale', and may suspect the forgery is such a *jeu d'esprit*. Haupt reprints the forgery (pp. 58–62); it may also be found in Wernsdorf, p. 178 *et sq.*

---

[1] Schenkl, p. 390 *et sq.*   [2] *Ibid.*   [3] Cf. Schenkl, p. 394 *et sq.*

A. *Editions of the* Halieutica

In the year 1534 G. Logus produced the Aldine *editio princeps*, which proclaimed 'hoc uolumine continentur poetae tres egregii' (i.e. Grattius, Ovid, and Nemesianus). This small book was based on the work done by Sannazaro. In his preface, Logus recounts how he was given a version[1] by a Silesian count named Aesiander, and we may attribute to the limitations imposed by working on that version the lack of progress in this edition.

The next significant edition was that of the learned Conrad Gesner of Zurich in 1556. Gesner was a renowned naturalist, and it was to be expected that he should make great advances in the criticism of the *Halieutica*. Strangely enough it was his grammatical criticism that was of the most importance. He drew attention to the false quantities in *anthias* (46) and *pompile* (101). Birt was the first later writer to comment on the latter, but even the learned Birt overlooked the former, and it was not until this century[2] that A. E. Housman paid attention to it!

The work of 'Hercules Ciofanus, Sulmonensis', which appeared at Antwerp in 1582, is good. (This is the second, enlarged, edition.) It contains valuable material derived from Octavius Pantagathus, and the ideas of Muret, the younger Aldus, and Achilles Statius were available to the author. It is in this edition that the first notes of discontent with the style of our 'Ovid' are sounded.

The edition of Pierre Pithou (P. Pithoeus) the younger, which appeared in 1590 at Paris, offers little save inferior readings from B, and the notes are confined to a statement about the repetition of v. 52. (This is a difficult work to find in libraries if the reader is unaware of the fact that the title is *Epigrammata et poematia vetera*.) Bersman(n)us' conjectures and notes were often reprinted. I have read them in the 'third edition' (Leipzig, 1596).

---

[1] A conflation of A and Sannazaro's two versions? Cf. Schenkl, p. 393.

[2] Quicherat notes it in his *Thesaurus Poeticus*, however.

Worthy of special attention is the excellent edition (entitled
Venatio novantiqua) published at Leyden in 1645, the work of
Jan van Vliet (I shall use his latinized name, Vlitius). In many
respects his edition approaches the ideal, and, taken by and
large, may be pronounced the most balanced that has been
published. Vlitius, however, was convinced, on insufficient
evidence, that Grattius was the author of the *Halieutica*, and
this idea occasionally distorts his comments. The emendations
proposed, and the notes, are worth careful study. I am of the
opinion that Vlitius' proposals have not been sufficiently
considered by later editors (e.g. his notes on 44, 80, 115).

A second Dutch critic, the younger Heinsius, issued an
edition in Amsterdam in 1661. It is needless to say that the
emendations are occasionally brilliant (e.g. *ciue*, v. 18), but
the lustre of his work is dimmed by the weight[1] given to the
Ms. B, the insistence that Ovid was the author, and the consequent editing by Ovidian standards. I also feel that he was not
sufficiently acquainted with the subject matter of the poem.
His notes are best read in the compendious edition of the elder
Burman, who had access, as he states in his preface, to a large
amount of material that Heinsius had not succeeded in incor-
porating in later editions. Burman seems to have printed this
just as it stood in the form of marginal queries. Burman's
edition (Amsterdam, 1727)[2] is a monument of industry, and it
collects masses of material in a convenient form, but the critical
work done on the text is not remarkable.

In 1780 J. C. Wernsdorf published at Altenburg the first
volume of his *Poetae latini minores*. It contains the *Halieutica*.
He has little textual criticism to add to that of his predecessors.
He devotes considerable attention to an elaboration of Vlitius'
theory about the authorship. He has a tendency to indulge in
ingenious speculation.

There is a welcome relief from ingenuity in the edition of
Haupt (Leipzig, 1838), which, for the first time in the history
of the text, made an *apparatus* available to scholars. Haupt has a
good, exact, introduction which gives a wealth of detail about

[1] 'quicquid in recensione huius fragmenti castigauimus, id codici Thuaneo ...
debetur'—not to be taken quite literally.
[2] The edition of 1713 has no notes.

the various Mss. He has also some important critical remarks
on the *Halieutica* in which he pioneered the study of vocabulary
and style in our poem. It is significant to note that he seems
uneasy about the authorship, for he goes to the trouble of
refuting a theory he puts forward himself: that the *Halieutica*
might have been concocted, with the aid of the indications in
Pliny, long after the time of Ovid. He finally concludes in
favour of the Ovidian authorship.

Merkel in his edition of the works of Ovid (Leipzig, 1851)
included the *Halieutica*, but the text is unsatisfactory, and in his
later edition of 1884 he omitted it. In Riese's edition of Ovid
(Leipzig, 1874) the *Halieutica* is also included and the treatment
is fairly good, being characterized by resolute common sense
rather than any flashes of insight.

It was in 1878, at Berlin,[1] that the youthful and exuberant
Theodor Birt published his *De Halieuticis Ovidio poetae falso
adscriptis*, and it is hard to see how this work can ever be second
to any other dealing with the same subject. This book has more
than 200 pages and brings a tremendous volume of learning to
the subject. There is fare of all sorts for the reader. The language, metre, style, and sources of the poem are subjected to
exhaustive examination. Birt came with great assurance to the
view that the poem was not written by Ovid, but should be
attributed to the age of Nero. He adduces a wealth of arguments for his theory, and concludes his work with a revised
text of the poem. Nothing published before, or since, gives an
editor anything like the help that Birt affords.

Yet, no sooner had Birt published this mighty work than
many critics assailed his views, and they have had their
arguments accepted as orthodox doctrine down to the present,
with few dissentient voices. The cause of this must be princi-
pally sought in the deficiencies of Birt's work. He has a plethoric
manner of dealing with his subject that leaves his reader unable
to see the wood for the trees. On the slightest provocation he
indulges in long digressions on various emendations suggested
by him for texts that are quoted incidentally in his argument.
Not only does he resemble Herodotus in his disposition of
matter but also in his lack of critical insight. He has proposed

---

[1] A portion was printed separately as a Marburg Doctoral Dissertation.

some of the most audacious conjectures that have ever been essayed for this text, and, instead of suggesting them in a tentative manner, he urges them with dogmatic assurance. Few things cloud the reader's judgment more than the facility with which Birt emends any text to fit in with his arguments.

Since then there has been no lack of editions of the *Halieutica*, but I do not think that the full fruits of Birt's work have been reaped by any successor. G. M. Edward's edition in Postgate's *Corpus*[1] has little new; Curcio's edition of 1902[2] is careless. Vollmer's edition (Leipzig, 1911) in the *Poetae latini minores* is careful, but the criticism is vitiated by the anxiety to vindicate Ovid's authorship. Owen's edition (Oxford, 1915) is undistinguished, and seems to be hasty and ill-considered. Ripert's edition of 1937 (Paris) is uncritical, and has a text of astonishing antiquity. It has a French translation and a few notes identifying the fish names. There are useful references in Lenz's introduction to his edition which was published at Turin in 1939 (2nd edition, little altered, 1956). I must, however, state that the work contains some inaccuracies in matters of fact.

The standard texts of the *Halieutica* were reprinted many times in complete editions of Ovid. I have not attempted to give an exhaustive list of such titles in my bibliography.

B. *General*

As fish was a much more important article of diet in ancient times than in modern, references to fish are scattered all through ancient literature. In particular, the Middle Comedy, which made fishmongers one of its favourite targets, abounded in allusions to fish.

Writers on certain scientific subjects had occasionally to describe fish: the physicians[3] when prescribing diets; the lexicographers[4] when glossing strange words; and, of course,

---

[1] Vol. 1 (London, 1894).   [2] *Poeti latini minori*, vol. 1 (Acireale).

[3] Especially Hippocrates (ed. Ermerins, Utrecht, 1859–64; Littré, Paris, 1839; the *CMG* ed. is not yet complete) and Galen (ed. Kühn, Leipzig, 1822–33; the *CMG* ed. is not yet complete); cf. Pliny 32 and Celsus.

[4] Cf. *Index Verborum et Rerum* s.v. *Etymologies*; Marx's *Lucilius*, p. lii; the arrangement of Athenaeus' *Deipnosophists* 7; and the dissertation of A. Papendick mentioned in the *Index Bibliographicus*.

the cooks.[1] The scientific study of ichthyology in antiquity, however, was mainly contained in the Aristotelian[2] works on animals: the five treatises which survive contain an amazing bulk of accurate observations, some details of which were not verified until the nineteenth century. The very excellence of Aristotle's work seems to have discouraged further purely scientific advance. His surviving and lost works on animals were rearranged and condensed into four books for popular reading by Aristophanes of Byzantium. An epitome of the first two books survives,[3] but this epitome does not contain any information about fish.

In accordance with Alexandrian taste, after the time of Aristotle ichthyology was handed over to encyclopedists, paradoxographers,[4] and poets. The surviving works of Pliny[5] (*Natural History*, 9 and 32), Athenaeus[6] (*Deipnosophists*, especially 7), and Aelian[7] (*De Natura Animalium* and *Varia Historia*) present us with a strange farrago of science, literature, and superstition, derived from lost authorities. We are fortunate that the *Halieutica* of Oppian survived the wreck of antiquity. This epic poet compiled five books of learning and legend about fishing which completely supplanted the similar works of Numenius and others (cf. Birt, p. 103 *et sq.*). He wrote in a pleasantly bright, but somewhat facile, style.[8]

After Aristotle the philosophers seem to have been interested in animals not for their own sake but for their use as pieces of evidence to support the doctrines of the school. In particular, a controversy raged between the Stoics and Academics whether animals possessed the faculty of reason, and echoes of this

---

[1] They are not very significant for our purposes.

[2] The ninth book of the *Historia Animalium* is especially rich in fish lore, but it has been doubted whether it is a genuine work of Aristotle's. (Gercke, *RE* 2.1047 and Christ—Stählin—Schmid, *Geschichte der Griechischen Literatur*[6], *Erster Teil*, p. 734.)

[3] This epitome, by Constantinus Porphyrogennetus, may be read in the *Supplementum Aristotelicum*, vol. i, pars i, ed. S. Lambros (Berlin, 1885).

[4] Cf. Antigonus Carystius in O. Keller's *Rerum naturalium scriptores graeci minores* (Leipzig, 1877).

[5] Ed. Jahn–Mayhoff (Leipzig, 1892–1909).

[6] Ed. G. Kaibel (Leipzig, 1887–90); F. Jacobs (Jena, 1832).

[7] Ed. R. Hercher (Leipzig, 1864–6).

[8] In addition to Mair's edition (see *Index Bibliographicus*), note those of J. G. Schneider[2] (Leipzig, 1813), and F. S. Lehrs (in *Poetae bucolici et didactici* (Paris, 1862)). For scholia, cf. Keydell, *RE* 18.703.

conflict are to be heard in the interesting work by Plutarch entitled *De Sollertia Animalium,* which contains several anecdotes found in our text, in Aelian, and in Oppian.[1]

During the last seventy-odd years several modern works of importance have appeared, which are of use in elucidating the *Halieutica.* I should award pride of place to *A Glossary of Greek Fishes,* a delightful work of good taste and polymath learning, by D'Arcy Wentworth Thompson (London, 1947). E. de Saint-Denis[2] published in Paris in the same year his *Le vocabulaire des animaux marins en latin classique,* which is a useful, accurate and sober book. Earlier works[3] which should be consulted are those of H. J. Cotte (see *Index Bibliographicus*), and G. Schmid (see *Index Bibliographicus*), who deals specifically with our poem, and has much useful information conveniently arranged, although, in my opinion, the wrong conclusions are drawn from it. The limitations of the former work are indicated by de Saint-Denis in his review (*REA* 47 (1945), p. 282 *et sq.*). The dissertation of A. Papendick has useful information that I have not been able to obtain elsewhere (see *Index Bibliographicus*). The work of R. Strömberg (see *Index Bibliographicus*) does not seem to contain much of use to an editor of this poem.

[1] C. Hubert has recently edited the *De Sollertia Animalium* in the *Moralia,* vol. vi, fasc. i (Leipzig, 1954). For the controversy, cf. Pohlenz, *Die Stoa,* i, 84.

[2] For various articles of importance by de Saint-Denis see *Index Bibliographicus.*

[3] O. Keller's *Antike Tierwelt* (see *Index Bibliographicus*) is a good general work.

HALIEVTICON

. . . .
accepit mundus legem. dedit arma per omnes,
admonuitque sui. uitulus sic †manuque† minatur,
qui nondum gerit in tenera iam cornua fronte,
sic dammae fugiunt, pugnant uirtute leones,
et morsu canis, et caudae sic scorpius ictu,   5
concussisque leuis pinnis sic euolat ales —
omnibus ignotae mortis timor, omnibus hostem
praesidiumque datum sentire, et noscere teli
uimque modumque sui — sic et Scarus arte sub undis
si n.   10
decidit, adsumptaque dolos tandem pauet esca,
non audet radiis obnixa occurrere fronte:
auersus crebro uimen sub uerbere caudae
laxans subsequitur, tutumque euadit in aequor.

   quin etiam si forte aliquis, dum praenatat, arcto   15
mitis luctantem scarus hunc in uimine uidit,
auersi caudam morsu tenet, atque †lita†. . . . . .
liber, seruato quem texit ciue, resultat.

   Sepia tarda fugae, tenui cum forte sub unda
deprensa est, iamiamque manus timet illa rapacis,   20
inficiens aequor nigrum uomit illa c⟨ruorem⟩
auertitque uias, oculos frustrata sequentis.

   clausus rete Lupus, quamuis inmitis et acer,
dimotis cauda submissus sidit arenis,
. . . . .in auras   25
emicat, atque dolos saltu deludit inultus.

   et Murena ferox, teretis sibi conscia tergi,
ad laxata magis conixa foramina retis,
tandem per multos euadit lubrica flexus,
exemploque nocet: cunctis iter inuenit una.   30

   at contra scopulis crinali corpore segnis

APPARATVS

Titulus. Ouidius . . . in eo uolumine quod Halieuticon inscribitur, *Plin. nat.*
$\overline{32}$.11; INCIP VERSVS OVIDI DE PISCIB; ET FERIS *A.*

1 *ante uersum lacunam indicauit Logus* accepit] praecepit *Birt* per] fere
Heinsius post mundus *interpunxit Vollmer*   2 manuque] namque *Sann.*,
nempe *Burmannus,* magna *Baehrens,* manca *Vollmer* minatur] minaci *Logus,*
Vlitius   3 qui] quae *Vlitius* nondum *Sann.*, nundum *A* in tenera
(*corr. ex* in tenerco)] intentat *Vlitius,* intentans *O. Skutsch* (*cum* quae)   4
dammae *Sann.*, dammate *A* et *post* fugiunt *habet A, del. Sann.* uirtute]
rictuque *Heinsius*   5 morsu *Sann.*, morou *A* scorpius *Sann.*, seurpius *A*
6 concussisque *Sann.*, cum cursisque *A* ales *Sann.*, alis *A*   7 omnibus
ignotae *Sann.*, Omnib: sic nocte *A,* omnibus innatus *Burmannus*   8 praesidi-
umque] perniciemque *Birt* sentire *Sann.*, sintire *A*   9 est *post* sui *addidit*
Riese   10 Sin *A*: nassae *uel sim. latere statuerunt edd.*   11 decidit]
incidit *Gesner, Heinsius* adsumpta. . .esca *K. Schenkl,* adsumpta. . .escan *A,*
adsumptam (assutam *Vlitius, Heinsius*). . .escam *Sann.* dolos *Baehrens,* dolo
(*an* dalo?) *A,* bolo *Heinsius* tandem pauet] depauit ut *Heinsius*   12
occurrere fronte *B*(obc-), occurre feronte *A*   13 auersus] auersae
Heinsius uimen *B,* uimens *A* sub] sed *Sann.* caudae *B* (caude), caudet *A*
14 aequor *B* (equor), equore *A*   15 aliquis] alius *Heinsius,* alius qui
Birt dum praenatat arto (arcto *Haupt*) *Heinsius,* dampronatareto *A,*
dum pone nataret *Gesner, Pantagathus,* dum pronatat extra *Vlitius,* damna
notarit *Birt*   16 mitis] intus *Riese*   17 lita] citatim *uel* citate
ego tentem, citato *Riese,* ita uellit *Vollmer,* ita tandem *Heinsius,* ita flexu
Vlitius   18 liber (uindex *K. Schenkl*) seruato quem texit (*uel* traxit
uel rexit) ciue *Heinsius,* Vberrer uato quem texit q: *A,* uerbere
seruato quem texit ciue *Riese,* liberiore natans quem texit nassa
Vlitius, alii alia resultat *Codex Ambros. S 81 sup., Vlitius, Heinsius,* resultet *A*
19 Sepia *B,* Saepia *A* fugae *Sann.,* fuge *A*   20 illa] hilla *Birt* rapacis
Sann., rapetis *A*   21 illa cruorem *Sann.,* illac *A,* ore cruorem *Achilles*
Statius, alii alia   22 sequentis] sequentes *Logus*   23 inmitis *Sann.*
(imm-), inmittis *uel sim. priore* t *dubia A,* immanis *Logus*   24 dimotis]
corr. ex Demotis *A* submissus *B,* submisus *A,* 'uix . . . subnisus' *Vollmer*
sidit *Pantagathus,* redet *A*   25 *priori continuat A*   26 atque *bis*
habet A, semel B saltu] astu *Birt* deludit *Sann.,* diludit *A* inultus] inultos
Sann.   27 et] at *Birt* (*p. 70*) murena *Sann.,* more *A* teretis sibi
Sann., et retis ibi *A* tergi *Sann.,* teri *A*   28 conixa *spreuit Haupt,*
accepit K. Schenkl, connextat *A,* conuexa *Haupt,* conuersa *Sann.* foramina
Sann., formi *A*   30 que *Sann.,* qui *A* nocet] nocens *Sann.* iter inuenit
Bersmannus, interuienit *A,* interuenit *Sann.*   31 scopulis *Sann.,* scupolis *A*

Polypus haeret, et hac eludit retia fraude;
et sub lege loci sumit mutatque colorem,
semper ei similis quem contegit; atque ubi praedam
pendentem saetis auidus rapit, hic quoque fallit,   35
elato calamo cum demum emersus in auras
brachia dissoluit, populatumque expuit hamum.
    at Mugil cauda pendentem euerberat escam,
excussamque legit. Lupus acri concitus ira
discursu fertur uario (fluctusque furentem   40
prosequitur), quassatque caput, dum uulnere saeuus
laxato cadat hamus, et ora patentia linquat.
    nec proprias uires nescit Murena nocendi
auxilioque sui......................   44a
............morsu nec comminus acri   44b
deficit, aut animos ponit captiua minacis.   45
Anthias †his† tergo, quae non uidet, utitur armis,
uim spinae nouitque suae, uersoque supinus
corpore lina secat, fixumque intercipit hamum.

CETERA, quae densas habitant animalia siluas,
aut uani quatiunt semper lymphata timores,   50
aut trahit in praeceps non sana ferocia mentis.
[ipsa sequi natura monet uel comminus ire]
    inpiger ecce Leo uenantum sternere pergit
agmina, et aduersis infert sua pectora telis!
quoque uenit fidens magis et sublatior ardet   55
(concussitque toros et uiribus addidit iram),
....
†prodedit† atque suo properat sibi robore letum.
    foedus Lucanis prouoluitur Vrsus ab antris,
quid nisi pondus iners, stolidique........
....
actus Aper saetis iram denuntiat hirtis,   60
se ruit oppositi nitens in uulnera ferri,
pressus et emisso moritur per uiscera telo.
    altera pars fidens pedibus dat terga sequenti,
ut pauidi Lepores, ut fuluo tergore Dammae,
et capto fugiens Ceruus sine fine timore.   65
....

32 haeret *Sann.*, heret *A*   hac *Sann.*, haec *A*   **33** et sub (pressus *Birt*, quod sub *K. Schenkl*) . . . . . sumit mutatque] ut sub . . . . . . sumat mutetque *Hemsterhusius (ad Lucian. dial. marin. 4.3)*   **34** praedam *Sann.*, p̄daret *A*   **35** saetis *Riese*, setis *A*   **36** cum] tum *Codex Ambros. S 81 sup., fort. recte.*   **37** brachia *Sann.*, bracha *A*   hamum *Sann.*, amum *A*   **39** conịctus *Sann.*, contịcitatur *A*   ira] aere *Vlitius*   **40** discursu *Sann.*, Discussu *A*   furentem *O. Skutsch*, ferentes *A*   **41** prosequitur] persequitur *Codex Ambros. S 81 sup.*   uulnera saeuus] uolnera saeuos, *et simm. ubique, Vollmer*   **42** hamus *Sann.*, amus *A*   **43** murena *Sann.*, morena *A*   **44** auxilioque sui] *post haec uerba lacunam indicauit Vlitius*, auxiliique sui *Haupt*, auxiliumque sui *Heinsius*, auxiliumque suum *Postgate*, auxilioque sibi *Logus*   morsu] *ex* uersu *corr. A*   comminus *Sann.*, cominus *A*   **45** *post hunc uersum lacunam indicauit Birt*   **46** his] in *Vollmer*, ast *Heinsius* tergo (tergi *Heinsius apud Burmannum*) quae non uidet *Sann.*, tergo quae (quae, *ut uidetur, ex* quite *corr.*) non uidit *A*, tergo quae concutit *uel* continet *Heinsius*   **47** nouitque suae *Sann.*, mouet quae sua et *A*   **48** lina secat *Sann.*, linas egat *A*   hamum *Sann.*, amum *A* *post hunc uersum lacunam indicauit Heinsius*   **49–81** *interpolatos censet Merkel*   **49–82** *damnauit Ciofanus*   **49** cetera *Sann.*, Et cetera *A*, at fera *Heinsius* siluas *Sann.*, silus *A*   **51** trahit in praeceps *Sann.*, trabit In preceps *A*   non sana] insana *Castiglioni (apud Lenz)*, uaesana *Lenz* ferocia mentis *Sann.*, ferotia mestes *A*   **52** *hunc uersum hic errore iteratum statui* ipsa] illa *Postgate*, saepta *Birt*   sequi] quati *Merkel*, peti *K. Schenkl monet*] mouet *Logus, sed ad 65 a* docet   comminus *editio Aldina a Gryphio iterata anno 1537:* conminus *A, sed cf. 65a* ire *Sann.*, ira.er. (*sed* irter *simile*) *A*   **55** quoque] quaque *Heinsius apud Burmannum*, quomque *K. Schenkl* uenit] sibi *K. Schenkl* sublatior *Sann.*, sibi latior *A*   **56** addidit *Sann.*, addit *A* *post hunc uersum lacunam indicauit Baehrens*   **57** prodedit] proruit *Gesner*, prosilit *uel* prodidit *Sann.*, prodigus *Vlitius*, procidit *Burmannus*, prodigit (*sc.* uires) *Vollmer*   **58** ursus *Sann.*, orsus *A*   **59** stolidique] stolidaeque *Sann.* *lacunam indicauit O. Skutsch*, ferotia mentis (*A*) *in uncis posuit Postgate qui* audacia cordis *in apparatu tentauit*, ferocia menti *Aldus Aldi N.*   **60** saetis *Sann.* (setis), retis *A*   denuntiat hirtis *Sann.*, denuntiate hireis *A*, (dum nuntiat *uel* dum concitat *Heinsius*)   **61** se ruit *Heinsius*, Seruit *A*, et ruit *Sann.*, sed ruit *Birt*   **62** Pressus *B*, Praessus *A* emisso *B*, emiso *A*, immisso *Heinsius*, fortasse eniso *O. Skutsch*   **64** dammae *Sann.*, demmae *A*   **65** capto] cauto *Heinsius*, idem *uel* rapido *Riese*   ceruus *Sann.*, aceruus *A*   *post hunc uersum lacunam indicaui*

ipsa sequi natura monet uel comminus ire.   65a
    hic generosus honos et gloria maior Equorum:
nam cupiunt animis palmam gaudentque triumpho,
seu septem spatiis circo meruere coronam
(nonne uides uictor quanto sublimius altum
adtollat caput, et uulgi se uenditet aurae?)   70
celsaue cum caeso decorantur terga leone
(quam tumidus, quantoque uenit spectabilis actu,
conspissatque solum generoso concita pulsu
ungula sub spoliis grauiter redeuntis opimis!)
    quin laus prima Canum, quibus est audacia praeceps,   75
uenandique sagax uirtus, uiresque sequendi.
quae nunc elatis rimantur naribus auram,
et nunc demisso quaerunt uestigia rostro,
et produnt clamore feram (dominumque uocando
increpitant), quam, si conlatis effugit armis,   80
insequitur tumulosque canis camposque per omnis.
. . . .
. . . . ⟨omnis⟩   81a
noster in arte labor positus, spes omnis in illa.
. . . .
nec tamen in medias pelagi te pergere sedes
admoneam, uastique maris temptare profundum:
inter utrumque loci melius moderabere finem   85
. . . .
aspera num saxis loca sin⟨t: nam⟩ talia lentos
deposcunt calamos, at purum retia litus;
num mons horrentes demittat celsior umbras
in mare: nam uarie quidam fugiuntque petuntque;
num uada subnatis imo uiridentur ab herbis: 90
⟨nam⟩. 90a
obiectetque moras, et molli seruiat algae.
    discripsit sedes uarie natura profundi,
nec cunctos una uoluit consistere pisces:
nam gaudent pelago quales Scombrique, Bouesque,
Hippuri celeres, et nigro tergore Milui,   95
et pretiosus Helops, nostris incognitus undis,
ac durus Xiphias, ictu non mitior ensis,
et pauidi magno fugientes agmine Thynni,

65a *hunc uersum abundare credidit Gesner, eiecit Vlitius* monet] docet *Logus*
com(m)inus ire *Sann.*, comminus irate *A*(*cf. u. 52*)   **66–74** *post 81*
O. Skutsch   **66** hic] hîc *Gesner*, hinc *Heinsius, qui postea (apud Bur-*
mannum ad u. 75) quid *legendum censuit*   **67** nam] iam *Heinsius* cupiunt
Birt, capiunt *A*   triumpho *Sann.*, triumfo *A   post hunc uersum aliquid*
excidisse censuit Vlitius   **70** aurae *Sann.*, aurate *A*   **71** Celsa *B* (*sed*
hoc in photographo legere nequeo), Caelsa *A*   caeso *Sann.*, cateso *A*   decorantur]
decoratur *Sann.*   leone] *nil hoc amplius legere possum*, leonem *uidit H. Schenkl*
72 quantoque uenit] quanto ueniat *Gesner, idem uel* quanto ut ueniat *Heinsius*
73 conspissatque *Sann.*, Conpiscatque (*ex* Conpsscatque *corr.*) *A*, conpescitque
K. Schenkl, conpescatque *Sann.*, concutiatque (*sed et apud Burm.* discutiatque
uel dispergatque) *Heinsius*, conculcatque *Bochartus (apud Burm.)*, conquas-
satque *Haupt*, conpisatque *Maurenbrecher (ThLL 3.2074.30)*, constipatue
uel conpressatue *O. Skutsch*, concrispatque *Birt*   generoso *Sann.*, generosso *A*
74 ungula sub spoliis *Sann.*, Vinculas abspoliis *A*   redeuntis *Sann.*, redeunte *A*
75 quin *Birt*, Qui *A*, quae *Logus*, quid *Sann.*, *idem uel* dein *Heinsius*   **76**
sagax *Sann.*, sacax *A*   **77** auram *Haupt*, aurara (*ut credo*) *A*, auras *Sann.*
78 et] at *Vollmer* quaerunt *Sann.*, querunt *A*   **80** quam *scripsi*,
quem *A*, quae *Vlitius*   **81** campos *ex* campis *corr. A* omnis] o̅m̅s *A*
81a *lacunam detexit Birt*, omnis *suppleuit O. Skutsch*   **82** *lacunam latere*
post hunc uersum censuit Ciofanus   **84** temptare] temp.l.tare *A*   **85**
inter] In‡' (‡' *supra lineam secunda, ut puto, manu scriptum*) *A*   loci *Sann.*, coci
A   moderabere *Sann.*, moderauere *A* finem] linum *Merkel*, funem
Bersmannus   post hunc uersum lacunam latere statuit Haupt   **86–87** *post*
89 *Birt*   **86** num] non *Pitheous* sint nam talia *Sann.*, sin   talia *A*
87 at] ccct *sim. in A*   purum *Sann.*, puerum *A*   **88** num] non *Heinsius*
(*ad 91*)   horrentes *Sann.*, orrentes *A*, torrentes *Riese*   umbras] undas *Riese*
89 uarie *B* (*sed hoc in photographo legere nequeo*), uariae *A*   quidam] quaedam
Birt   **90** num] non *Heinsius   post hunc uersum lacunam indicauit Sann.* (nam
suppleui)   **91** obiectetque *Heinsius*, Oblectetque *A*   molli seruiat algae
(algate *A*) *Sann.*, mollis uestiat alga *Merkel*   **92** discripsit] descripsit
Sann.   uarie *Codex Ambros. S 81 sup.*, uariae *A*, uarias *Sann.*   **93** cunctos
corr. ex conctos *A*   **94** quales] squali *uel* squatinae *Vlitius*, late *Casti-*
glioni (apud Lenz)   **95** hippuri celeres] hippurique leues, *nescio quis in*
margine Aldinae editionis quae in Museo Britannico seruatur, hippuri et celeres
Ehwald   tergore milui *Sann.*, tergoret mihi (*an* milii?) *A*, tergore iuli
Lachmann, ad Lucr. 6.552   **96** et] at *Burmannus, errore typ., ut uidetur*
pretiosus *Sann.*, praetiosus *A*   helops] elops *Sann.*   **97** durus] duro
Sann.   ensis *Sann.*, hensis *A*   **98** thynni *Birt*, thinni *A*, thunni *Sann.*

parua Echenais (at est, mirum, mora puppibus ingens),
tuque, comes ratium tractique per aequora sulci,   100
qui semper spumas sequeris, Pompile, nitentes.

. . . .

Cercyrosque ferox scopulorum fine moratur,
Cantharus ingratus suco, tum concolor illi
Orphus, caeruleaque rubens Erythinus in unda,
insignis Sargusque notis, insignis Iulis,   105
et super aurata Sparulus ceruice refulgens,
et rutilus Phager, et fului Synodontes, et ex se
concipiens Channe, gemino non functa parente,
tum uiridis squamis paruo Saxatilis ore,
et rarus Faber, et pictae Mormyres, et auri   110
Chrysophrys imitata decus, tum corporis Vmbrae
liuentis, rapidique Lupi, Percaeque, Tragique,
quin laude insignis caudae Melanurus, et ardens
auratis Murena notis, Merulaeque uirentes,
inmitisque suae Cancer per uulnera genti,   115
et capitis duro nociturus Scorpios ictu,
ac numquam aestiuo conspectus sidere Glaucus.

  at contra herbosa pisces luxantur arena,
ut Scarus, epastas solus qui ruminat escas,
fecundumque genus Menae, Lamirosque, Smarisque,   120
atque inmunda Chromis, merito uilissima Salpa,
atque auium dulces nidos imitata sub undis
. . . .
et squa⟨mas⟩ tenui suffusus sanguine Mullus,
fulgentes Soleae candore, et concolor i⟨llis⟩
Passer, et Adriaco mirandus litore Rhombus,   125
tum Lepores lati, tum molles tergore Ranae,
extremi †pareuc†. . . . .
. . . .
. . . .
lubricus, et spina nocuus non Gobius ulla,   130
et nigrum niueo portans in corpore uirus
Lolligo, durique Sues, sinuosaque Caris,
et tam deformi non dignus nomine Asellus,
tuque, peregrinis, Acipenser, nobilis undis.

99 echenais *Sann.* (-eis *secundis curis*), echena ir *A*   at est *Haupt*, adest *A*
100–101 *pos t*117 *Birt*   **100** comes *Sann.*, comis *A*   ratium *corr. ex*
ratiom *A*   **101** pompile *Sann.*, pomphile *A*   nitentes] *an* natantes?
Birt, p. 30   post uersum lacunam indicaui   **102** moratur] *fortasse* morantur,
moratus *Sann.*   **103** ingratus] et gratus *spreuit Birt*   **104** orphus
Vlitius, Orphas *A*, orphos *Sann.*   caerulea *Sann.*, caerolea *A*   erythinus *Sann.*,
erithinus (e *ex* l *corr.*) *A*   **105** que *Sann.*, qui *A*   Iulis *Birt*,
·I·alis *A*, et alis *Sann.*   **106** superaurata *uno uerbo Heinsius*
107 phager *Haupt*, harcer *A*, pager *Sann.*   synodontes *Sann.*,
synodantes *A*   **108** channe *Sann.*, channem *A*   non functa
parente *scripsi*, sibi fundata parente (*an* riasente?) *A*, fraudata parente
Sann., (gemini) uice functa parentis *Haupt*, sine facta parente *K. Schenkl*,
sibi iuncta parenti *Birt*, sic functa parente *spreuit Birt, accepit Edwards*, sibi
functa parente *Curcio*   **110** rarus faber *Sann.*, raru fauer *A*   pictae
mormyres *Sann.*, pietate murmires *A*   **111** umbrae *Sann.*, ūbre *A*
112 liuentis *Sann.*, liuentes *A*   percae *Sann.*, percate *A*   **113** quin
laude] nigrore *O. Skutsch*, quid laude *Heinsius, ad 75*   caudae *Sann.*, caudate
A   **114** murena *Sann.*, munera *A*   merulae *Sann.*, merolate *A*   **115**
inmitisque *Sann.* (imm-), Imitisque *A*, infamisque *Haupt* (*Opusc. i.209*),
intutusque *Riese* cancer] conger *Sann.*, gonger *Vollmer*   genti *Vlitius*,
gentes (*ex* gentei *correctum, ut putat Vollmer*) *A*, gentis *Sann.*   **116** capitis]
captus *Ciacconus* duro] diro *Birt*   nociturus *Sann.*, noxiturus *A*   scorpios
Sann., scorpio *A*   ictu *Sann.*, Iet *corr. in* Ict *A*   **117** aestiuo *Sann.*,
stiuo *A*   *in A spatium post* ac *relictum est*   **118** luxantur *Haupt, dubitanter*,
laxantur *A*, laetantur *spreuit Vlitius, accepit Riese*   **119** scarus *Sann.*,
carus (ca *supra lineam, secunda, ut uidetur, manu scriptum*) *A*   ruminat *Sann.*,
ruminet *A*   **120** fecun *supra lineam, secunda, ut uidetur, manu scriptum*
in A   menae *Sann.*, menate *A*   **121** inmunda *Sann.* (imm-), In unda
A   **122** atque] *fortasse* quaeque *O. Skutsch, Kenney* dulces] phycis
Vlitius (*iam Gesner, p. 69*)   *lacunam post hunc uersum posuerunt Gesner et Panta-*
gathus   **123** squamas *Aldus Aldi N.*, squa *A*, squatus et *Vlitius*, squalus
et *Sann.*, squalus *Logus*, squatina et *Birt*   sanguine mullus *Sann.*, sanguiṣ
nemulas *A*   **124** soleae *Sann.*, soleate (t *ex* c *corr.*) *A*   concolor illis
Logus, concolori *A*, concolor illi *Sann.*   **125** Adriaco] Hadriaco *Sann.*
rhombus *Sann.*, rumbus (b *super* p, *et, ut uidetur,* t *scripta*) *A*   **126** tum
(*priore loco*) *Sann.*, Tunc *A*, hinc *Merkel*   lati *Sann.*, leti *A*   ranae *Sann.*,
rante *A*   **127, 128, 129** *post* pareuc *nil in A* (*hoc spatio relicto*)
130 gobius *Codex Ambros. S 81 sup.*, gouius *A*   ulla (*ut credo, sed Vollmer:*
'ullus, *sic, an* ullis? *A*')] ulli *Vollmer*, ulta *Birt*, una *Housman*   **131** *scriba*
post hunc uersum relinquere lacunam uoluisse uidetur: nunc prima uersus 132 littera
maior est quam aliae primae   **132** sinuosaque *Sann.*, sin uoraque (*aliquid*
post n *erasum est*) *A*   **133** asellus] *an* usellus *habet A?*   **134**
acipenser *Sann.*, accipiens er *A*.

carminis finis in A non indicatur.

COMMENTARY

TITLE: *Halieuticon* is most probably a neuter plural genitive like *Georgicon*. K.-E. Henriksson, in his *Griechische Büchertitel in der römischen Literatur* (*Annales Acad. Scient. Fennicae*, Ser. B, Tom. 102,1, Helsinki, 1956), accepts the form Ἁλιευτικά without discussion on p. 62. If the title were in the singular, one would expect the masculine form Ἁλιευτικός parallel to the Κυνηγετικός of ps.-Xenophon and Arrian (Henriksson, p. 64). The following titles in -ικόν are indexed by Henriksson: Εἰσαγωγικόν, Ὁδοιπορικόν, Προπεμπτικόν, Ὑπογνωστικόν, Ὑπομνηστικόν. In all these cases, either the titles may not be book-titles (as ours, according to Pliny (32.11), is), or it is not possible to be sure whether the nominative was masculine or neuter. There is often no extant example of the nominative case of a particular book title in the ancient authors (cf. Henriksson, p. 12). The loss of the Greek title was natural (cf. the *Apocolocyntosis* of Seneca), but it may be that the Ms. has been damaged, and that the title has been inferred from the contents.

1 ACCEPIT MUNDUS LEGEM: a close parallel to this expression is found in Manilius (1.85), *lingua suas accepit barbara leges* (cf. *M* 4.704, *accipiunt legem*, 'they accept the conditions'; *M* 10.50). *mundus* is most naturally taken to mean the 'world and all it contains', as in *M* 15.456. *legem* then is evidently a natural or cosmic law: cf. *T* 1.8.5, *omnia naturae praepostera legibus ibunt,* and *M* 15.71, etc.; and the whole phrase reads: 'the world accepted a law'. This is the Stoic idea that the world was God and laid down laws that bound itself and the creatures that formed part of it. Thus the passage in Lucan 2.9, *fixit in aeternum causas qua cuncta coercet, se quoque lege tenens,* and the scholium quoted in *SVF* 1.43.4, *hoc secundum Stoicos dicit qui adfirmant mundum prudentia ac lege firmatum, ipsumque deum esse sibi legem,* show that here we have an idea which must have been rather a philosophical commonplace in the schools.

DEDIT ARMA PER OMNES: for the notion here it is easy to compare *M* 10.546, *neue feras, quibus arma dedit natura, lacesse*. The subject in our text must clearly be *mundus*, but the introduction of *omnes* without any noun is awkward. It has been suggested by Logus, Burman, and Vollmer that the opening lines of the text are lost, and this theory must be accepted, because: (*a*) no explanation is given of *mundus* and *omnes*; (*b*) it is not stated what the *lex* is, and the word *accepit* implies that it has been stated, especially in its present emphatic position; (*c*) it is most unnatural to commence a work of this nature without a reference to the subject to be discussed; (*d*) it is not improbable that this loss of text may explain the loss of the title.

OMNES: supply *feras* or the like.

The unusual construction *dedit . . . per omnes*, seems first to be paralleled from the sixth-century[1] poet Luxorius in *Anth. Lat.* 287.14,

> [*uersus*] . . .
> *discretos titulis . . . per nostri similes*
> *dato sodales.*

The construction with local words is to be found in authors of the first century, however. In prose we find the passive: *sermo per totam ciuitatem est datus*, Liv. 2.2.4 (cf. Wulsch, G., *De praepositionis 'per' usu Liviano* (Halle, 1880), p. 33); and in poetry the active is to be seen: *Aen.* 8.30, *dedit per membra quietem*; Stat. *silu.* 3.3.23, *date serta per aras*, etc. In Paul. Fest. p. 378 M we read a gloss on Cato which says *uiritim dicitur dari, quod datur per singulos uiros*, but this, at the best, is hardly earlier than Festus. However, the passage from local to personal words is not so abrupt (constructions like *proficiscitur in Aeduos* (= *in fines Aeduorum*) should be noted), and it seems easier to believe that the text is correct than to adopt Heinsius' suggestion, *dedit arma. fere omnes admonuitque sui*; *fere* here would be an intolerable weakening of the point that the author is trying to make, and would directly contradict vv. 7–8; the elision of *fere* and the postponement of *que* would not be such strong arguments against the proposal, cf. v. 133 and vv. 47, 105. Birt (p. 12) asks why the author did not use the obvious *dedit omnibus arma*: the text is more emphatic, and *per* conveys an idea of distribution.

2 ADMONUITQUE SUI: Vollmer explains that *sui* means 'ut uirium suarum memores essent' (I do not agree when he claims 'non [potuit] scribi nisi a poeta sermonis peritissimo', cf. *RhM* 55 (1900), p. 529). The use may be illustrated by Cic. *nat. deor.* 2.124, *tantam ingenuit animantibus conseruandi sui natura custodiam.*[2] A good parallel comes from Stat. *Theb.* 11.746 [*leo, iam piger,*] *erigitur, meminitque sui;*

---

[1] Cf. Levy, *RE* 13.2102.

[2] The use of *sui* to refer to the logical subject is natural in such a context, and our text does not necessarily show Ovidian influence although this was 'a familiar earmark of Ovidian style' (cf. R. F. Thomason, *CPh* 19 (1924), p. 155). Cf. *ignoratio sui*, Seneca *dial.* 7.5.2.

cf. Seneca *Herc. F.* 808; Claud. *carm. min.* 49.17, *meminit captiua [torpedo] sui.*[1]

UITULUS SIC MANUQUE MINATUR: I believe that this passage down to v. 6 has been imitated from Lucretius 5.1034 *et sq.* (cf. *Atti*, p. 19). Even where there are differences in the examples, clues can be seen in the text of Lucretius. Thus *canis* (v. 5) may be suggested by *catuli*, and the extraordinary *nondum iam* in the next verse may be suggested by the *iam tum* of v. 1037 or the *uix iam* shown by the *Codex Oblongus* in the next verse. The *dammae* and *scorpius ictu* seem to be favourites of our author (cf. vv. 64, 116).

The first example given in our text was a commonplace with the poets:

> uituli nondum metuenda fronte minaces
>
> *A* 3.13.15
>
> . . . . . . *necdum firmatis cornibus audax*
> *iam regit armentum uitulus . . .*
>
> Claud. 8.384
>
> *uitulusque inermi fronte prurit in pugnam*
>
> Mart. 3.58.11
>
> *sic uitulus molli proelia fronte cupit*
>
> Mart. 6.38.8

cf. also

Juv. 12.7 *et sq.*,

> *uitulus . . . . . . quem iam pudet ubera matris*
> *ducere, qui uexat nascenti robora cornu*

Gratt. 489,

> *teneraque extrudens cornua fronte [haedus]*

Claud. *Rapt. Pros.* 1.127,

> *uitulam . . . . . . quae nondum proterit arua*
> *nec noua lunatae curuauit germina frontis*

(Stat. *Theb.* 6.267, *et nondum lunatis fronte iuuencis*)

Sen. *Tro.* 537,

> *sic ille magni paruus armenti comes*
> *primisque nondum cornibus findens cutem . . . . . .*
> *gregem paternum ducit ac pecori imperat (et ibid.* 1093).

SIC: cf. Appendix 1.

A difficult problem is raised by the corrupt word *manuque*. Sannazaro's *namque* has generally been adopted, but it involves a pleonasm, as either *sic* or *namque* would appear to be sufficient to introduce the clause. Now Löfstedt, in *Spätlateinische Studien*, p. 31,

[1] Cf. Plin. *nat.* 9.143, *nouit torpedo uim suam.* This is exactly the meaning here.

shows that rather similar pleonastic uses may be found in Vitruvius and other writers in the vulgar idiom, and we seem to be faced with a similar occurrence in *nondum iam* in the next line. However, as the text here does not show *namque*, and as the usage in the next line seems to show literary imitation, I think it is rash to import *namque* into the text here.

If *namque* were actually in the text I would believe that Burman was correct when he conjectured *nempe*, for the substitution of *namque* for *nempe* is common (cf. Housman on Manilius 2.741). None of the editors' conjectures convinces me, but I like Baehrens' *magna*.

3   QUI NONDUM GERIT IN TENERA IAM CORNUA FRONTE: it seems that here *nondum . . . iam* means simply *nondum*. Owen (*CQ* 8 (1914), p. 271) suggests that here we should take *nondum* with *gerit* and *iam* with *tenera*: 'who does not bear on his now tender forehead'. . . . Evidently Owen takes *iam* as *nunc* here! *iam* as 'already' would imply that the head of the calf became more sensitive before the horns began to sprout, but my friends inform me that this is not the case; *iam* as 'still' would seem to give permissible sense, but the context[1] usually has some word to make the meaning clear—cf. *ThLL* 7.107.60 and 7.108.20, and, e.g., *M* 11.144.

TENERA: without horns—cf. *inermi*, Mart. 3.58.11; *molli*, Mart. 6.38.8; and *teneraque extrudens cornua fronte*, Gratt. 489; thus Vlitius' *intentat* is not forced on us. If the text is to stand we have the choice of some not entirely convincing defences[2]: (*a*) we may have a simple pleonasm as explained *supra*, v. 2, on *sic namque*; (*b*) the phrase may be built on the analogy of *nondum etiam* (Plaut. Ter.) and *necdum etiam* (Cat. 64.55; Verg. *Aen.* 8.697; Ciris 146); or (*c*) our poet may have felt that the *iam tum* of Lucr. 5.1037 (or the *uix iam* seen in the *Codex Oblongus* at Lucr. 5.1038), was a similar pleonasm and thus imitated it (cf. Birt, p. 102).

As already indicated, I favour the reason last set out above. Vlitius was so dissatisfied with the text that he suggested we should read

> *sic namque minaci*
> *quae nondum gerit intentat iam cornua fronte.*

This is an excellent conjecture, but before I could accept it I

---

[1] *nondum* in our context indicates the meaning 'already' for *iam*, as the two words are so often contrasted (cf. Birt, p. 14).

[2] There is no doubt that Varro *rust.* 2.2.2 should not read *iam nondum*. There are many examples indicated in Goetz' text where words have been erroneously repeated: *quod* 1.15, *et* 1.22.6, etc., etc. Baehrens has an interesting conjectural *nondum . . . tum* in Val. Flacc. 1.662. Hardly sufficient to defend our text, however!

should like definite evidence that some scribe did endeavour to correct our text, for only if this has happened can I understand how so radical a change could have taken place. O. Skutsch (c.f. *Ovidiana*, p. 445) restored the passage to read

sic usque minatur,
quae nondum gerit intentans iam cornua fronte
(or   *quae nondum genuit tentans iam cornua fronte*),

a reading which follows Vlitius in contrasting *nondum* and *iam*, and is well supported by Vergilian parallels: *usque minatur* (*Aen.* 2.628), and [*uitulus*] . . . *curuans iam cornua fronte* (*Geo.* 4.299).

  4 PUGNANT UIRTUTE LEONES: *uirtute* with *pugnant* is rather strange, for one would expect a word implying a part of the body, as in the parallel clauses following: *morsu canis, et caudae sic scorpius ictu.* Heinsius disposed of this difficulty by reading *pugnant rictuque leones*, a conjecture that neatly supplies a conjunction too. But the contrast is clearly with the timorous *dammae*, and the courage of the lion was proverbial (cf. Aristotle, 488 b 17; Plato, *Laches* 196DE; etc.); furthermore the asyndeton is in the manner of the author—cf. Appendix 1. We must retain the text.

  5 ET MORSU CANIS: here the construction is carried forward from the previous line, but there is a new contrast unhappily combined with the one we have just seen, for now the contrast is between the biting mouth of the hound, and the stinging tail of the scorpion. The discussion of the *uirtus* of the *leones* as distinct from the flight of the *dammae* is thus seen to be irrelevant to the exemplification of *dedit arma per omnes* (v. 1) which is here resumed. Further evidence of the clumsy nature of our author's work is to be seen in v. 3 which shows that the knowledge of self-defence is instinctive in animals—this idea seems to be lost sight of in vv. 4–6.

  ET CAUDAE SIC SCORPIUS ICTU: this is echoed in *capitis . . . scorpios ictu* (v. 115). The change in form in our text may be genuine and represent a distinction between the animal and the fish; it is not, however, improbable that either form is corrupt.

  6 CONCUSSISQUE . . . PINNIS: we talk of 'beating wings', and the ancients talk of 'clapping wings'. Thus we have *plausis . . . alis* M 14.507, M 14.577, and it seems that this phrase is imitated here. Claudian has (3.122) *concutit alas.*[1]

  LEUIS is used predicatively; EUOLAT: *e periculo*, I suppose. One might consider *auolat* more suitable, and it is palaeographically probable (cf. Prolegomena, p. 5).

---

[1] *penna* or *pinna*? Discussion on this point is as yet inconclusive. Cf. Bährens, *Sprachlicher Kommentar*, pp. 50–1; Sommer, *Kritische Erläuterungen*, pp. 15–16.

7 OMNIBUS IGNOTAE MORTIS TIMOR: cf. Seneca *Ep.* 121.19, *adparet illis [animalibus] inesse nocituri scientiam non experimento collectam, nam antequam possint experisci, cauent*; and also Pliny *nat.* 8.9–10.

IGNOTAE MORTIS, because they will have no knowledge of it before death (cf. 'that undiscovered country from whose bourne no traveller returns'). This use is analogous to *Aen.* 5.871, *nudus in ignota, Palinure, iacebis harena* (Servius, *ad loc.*, *peregrina, ante non uisa*); and *Aen.* 11.254, *ignota lacessere bella.* There is a deliberate contrast between death which is unknown, and their methods of self-defence which are so well known to them.

OMNIBUS . . . TIMOR: a rather unusual periphrasis for *timent omnes*, but cf. Stat. *Theb.* 12.171, *auditu turbatus ager, timor omnibus ingens.*

OMNIBUS HOSTEM: *omnis* is often repeated by the poets for emphatic effect; cf. *Aen.* 8.705–6; 10.804–5; 12.421–2; *Geo.* 3.480; *Aen.* 12.548–9; 8.718; *Geo.* 4.184; Gratt. 17; *M* 4.227; *M* 7.198; *Ep.* 8.75–6.

8 PRAESIDIUMQUE DATUM SENTIRE: cf. *F* 5.5, *posse datur diuersas reddere causas.* Birt (p. 102) fails to see the wood for the trees here: he insists that some notion of enmity or danger must be parallel to *hostem*, which he supplies by writing *perniciemque.* This is quite unnecessary. The whole emphasis of the context is on the fact that animals have instinctive knowledge of their means of defence. *sentire* is little more than *nouisse*—cf. Hor. *sat.* 2.2.31.

9 For UIM meaning power, cf. Cic. *Cael.* 58, *uimque eius [ueneni] esse expertum.* . . .

MODUM I should translate as 'limitation' or simply 'limit', for this seems closest to the root meaning of 'measure'. Cf. *T* 1.11.44, *ipse modum statuam carminis, illa sui.* 'Method of use', is not, however, an impossible meaning: Grattius 121, *omnia tela modi melius finxere salubres*, and *AA* 3.787, *mille modi Veneris.* Generally, for the idea and expression, cf. Plin. *nat.* 9.143, *nouit torpedo uim suam*; and v. 43, *inf.*; and notes on v. 2, *sup.*

SIC ET SCARUS: *sic* clearly introduces all the examples which follow, down to v. 48. Commentators generally agree that the examples all show that each animal has its own particular method of self-defence (*dedit arma per omnes*, v. 1). They believe that the series is continued down to v. 65, the animals in vv. 53–62 defending themselves with pugnacious bravery, and those in vv. 63–65 with discretion. I cannot agree with this view for several reasons: (*a*) the animals in vv. 53–62 seem all to cause their own destruction, not to protect themselves; (*b*) *sic* would not properly explain the statements that we have just read (vv. 8–9); (c) no rational connexion with vv. 66–81 follows from this theory. Hence I believe that we must see in vv. 9–65 a series of examples of the idea *accepit mundus legem* (v. 1) and *omnibus datum sentire et noscere*, because [*mundus*] *admonuit . . . sui* (v. 2). This is echoed later on by *nec proprias uires nescit murena nocendi* (v. 43) and *ipsa sequi natura monet uel comminus ire* (v. 52=65a). These considerations are developed *infra*, in the commentary on v. 65a.

It must be allowed that the examples down to v. 48 all set out particular methods by which fishes defend themselves, and lend some colour to the view that the *dedit arma per omnes* idea is, to some extent, present. All these passages, however, seem to have been translated carefully from the Greek (see parallels quoted by Lenz), and I believe that our author has rather unsatisfactorily built his thoughts around somewhat contradictory elements.

For the criticism of the following lines the parallel passages set out by Lenz in his edition are of the utmost importance.

ARTE: according to Birt (p. 78) this is the fisherman's art. I do not see how one can be sure—cf. *dolos* v. 11 and v. 26 where the fishermen are meant; and *fraude* (v. 32) and *fallit* (v. 35) where the guile of the *polypus* is meant.

10 For the lacuna cf. discussion in Prolegomena, p. 3. *Sin* in the Ms. probably represents *si nassa* or *si nassae* or the like, as editors claim, but I do not believe that the gap can be filled with any hope of certainty now.

11 DECIDIT is adequately supported by *AA* 2.2, *decidit in casses praeda petita meos* (cf. also *RA* 502). Consequently the idea of Gesner and Heinsius that we should read *incidit* (cf. Juv. 4.39, *incidit spatium . . . rhombi*) is unnecessary. Heinsius believes that *sin* in v. 10 is the remnant of a *varia lectio* '*incidit*'.

ADSUMPTAQUE DOLOS TANDEM PAVET ESCA: a comparison with Cassiodorus *uar.* 11.40.8, *scarus, esca pellectus, cum iunceum carcerem coeperit introire, mox se ad exitium suum inuitatum fuisse cognouerit, in caudam labitur, paulatim se ab angusto subducens*, makes me suspect that we should adopt Baehrens' reading here (cf. *Jenaer Literaturzeitung* 6 (1879), p. 252 *et sq.*): the *scarus* enters the net incautiously and then awakes to his danger as in Opp. 4.49 *et sq.*, εὖτε γὰρ ἐς κύρτοιο πέσῃ λόχον αἴολος ἰχθύς, αὐτίκ' ἐπεφράσθη τε καὶ ἐκδῦναι κακότητος πειρᾶται . . . . It would be odd to declare that the bait was feared—hence *adsumptam . . . escam* must be rejected. As Birt (p. 78) objected, when discussing K. Schenkl's *adsumptaque dolo . . . esca*, the *scarus* takes the bait not through guile, but through lack of it. It is easy to see how the position of *esca* would induce a scribe to read the accusative with *pauet*.

Vlitius suggests *assutam*. The bait, however, it seems, was smeared on the trap, or merely left lying in it (Plin. *nat.* 9.92, *nassis inlinuntur*; 10.194, *coiciuntur in nassas*; also *RE* cited on v. 12). A primary meaning of *adsumo* (*ThLL* 2.926.59) is 'to consume food or drink'.

TANDEM PAUET ESCA: this ending of the line is not in the manner of Ovid.[1] Heinsius' conjecture *depauit ut escam* is very improbable, however.

12 RADIIS: just inside the mouth of the *nassa* were several rods pointing so as to injure the eyes of the fish attempting to escape back through the entrance. Cf. Oppian 3.53 and the account of the *nassa* by 'Aug. Hug.' in *RE* 16.1793.

OBNIXA: as Birt points out (p. 36), this word is not found in Ovid.

OCCURRERE: evidently here means 'run against' or 'dash against'. I have not found this meaning in Ovid, but the Caesarian meaning of 'attack' seems substantially to be that we meet here (e.g. *ciu.* 1.40.4).

13 CREBRO: for this use in the singular with a plural implication, cf. *crebro uertice tortus Halys* (*EP* 4.10.48), etc.

SUB UERBERE CAUDAE LAXANS: as explained in Appendix 2, I take this phrase to qualify *uimen* and not *scarus*. This involves taking *laxans* as intransitive. It then becomes unnecessary to remove *sub* on the grounds of redundancy, so one has not to read a violently postponed *sed* in its place, as suggested by Sannazaro and others (cf. also Appendix 1).

UERBERE: this word is most common in the plural, but the singular was convenient for the poets, cf. Neue-Wagener, i.712. The phrase *uerbere caudae* may possibly be suggested by the *obscaenus sensus* in Hor. *sat.* 2.7.49 or by Lucan 1.208, and the use here has been imitated in Ausonius, *Mos.* 98. One should compare Tib. 1.5.3.

14 LAXANS: intransitive, cf. Appendix 2; any attempt to read a transitive sense, and take the word as qualifying *scarus*, will leave *subsequitur* most difficult to explain.

SUBSEQUITUR: 'following closely' the wickerwork as it loosens under the blows of his tail (cf. *subsequor ancillam furtim*, *Ep.* 19.131).

EUADIT: for the construction *euadere in*, cf. Cic. *nat. deor.* 2.95, *ex illis abditis sedibus euadere in haec loca.* . . .

15 QUIN ETIAM SI FORTE: for *quin etiam si*, cf. Plaut. *Cas.* 93, *quin edepol etiam si*, and Quint. *decl.* 281, p. 145.23. *si forte* is fre-

---

[1] For an epigraphic poem written about the time of Ovid which shows several abnormal endings of lines, cf. Norden, p. 437, n. 2.

quent in Ovid—*Ep.* 17.31, etc.; cf. also *quae si forte aliquid* . . .,
Prop. 2.22.11.

SI . . . ALIQUIS: 'if another' rather than 'if any'. There are two
points to be remarked: (*a*) *aliquis* is rare with *si* (cf., e.g. Draeger,
Ueber Syntax . . ., p. 7, and Uhlmann, p. 86) save when used emphatic-
ally and removed from the conjunction (cf. Stolz-Schmalz, p. 483).
As may be seen from Draeger, and Uhlmann, the usage was gradu-
ally creeping into the language. (*b*) The use of *aliquis* rather than
alius. It seems that the ancients were not so quick as we are to
distinguish 'any' from 'any other'. The confusion is usually regarded
as a sign of the vulgar tongue, and Löfstedt (*Beiträge*, p. 115) gives
instances of the usage from late Latin. So Sedgwick notes the usages
in Petronius 38.15 and 45.4, and remarks that Löfstedt did not
allude to these passages.[1] Now Vollmer in the *ThLL* (1.1608.74)
claims that *aliquis* can never have the force of *alius quis* although the
Glossaries translate it as ἕτερός τις and ἄλλος τις. Yet he quotes
several passages where it seems to me that the meaning of *alius quis*
is the more natural: Sen. *benef.* 5.10.2, *par sum, sed alicui—quis enim*
par est sibi?; Cic. *Brut.* 163, *uelim aliquid Antonio praeter illum* . . .
libellum . . . *libuisset scribere*; etc. Consequently I am of opinion that
Heinsius and Birt, when they substitute *alius* for *aliquis* here, are
being led astray by the instinct that deceived the scribes of the
codd. deteriores et interpolati at Cic. *de orat.* 2.170 and similar passages.
The adjectival form *aliquis* is usual (*ThLL* 1.1606.65).

DUM PRAENATAT ARCTO: this reading of Heinsius seems almost
certain. Birt (p. 81) points out that the distance of *arcto* from *uimine*
is an objection, but one may compare other passages in the poem
where the sense runs beyond the end of the line: *lentos deposcunt*
calamos (vv. 86–7); *uulnere saeuus laxato* (vv. 41–2, cf. Norden,
p. 399). We must take *praenatat* as 'swims by': the *scarus* is in the weel,
and as he looks out he sees his comrade 'swim (by) in front of him'.
The same idea may be seen in Pliny 9.146,[2] [*urtica*] *praenatante*
pisciculo frondem suam spargit—'as a little fish swims (by) in front of
it'—and Verg. *Aen.* 6.705, *Lethaeumque, domos placidas qui praenatat,*
amnem—'which floats (by), in front of the peaceful mansions'.
Cf. Tac. *Ann.* 2.6.4, *Rhenus* . . . *Germaniam praeuehitur*, where we
translate 'flows past', but the meaning is 'flows in front of'.[3] The
error in the Ms. may easily be explained. Both *pro* and *prae* were
written with similar *notae* (*N.L.*, p. 175 *et sq.*), and, in any event,

[1] Löfstedt, *Beiträge* (p. 113), shows that the same phenomenon is to be seen in
the use of *omnes* for *ceteri*.
[2] Contrast 9.186 'swimming ahead'.
[3] Full treatment by Blase in *WKPh* 33 (1916), cols. 280, 306.

there was a tendency in the later language to confuse compounds in *pro* and *prae* (cf. Stolz-Schmalz, p. 533). (*pronatare* does not give satisfactory sense—cf. Hyg. *Astr.* 2.17 where it means 'swim forth'.) The palaeographic history must be like this:

dum praenatat arcto	(Haupt's orthography)
dam ⎫	(cf. Prolegomena, p. 5)
pronatat areto ⎬	(e for c: cf. Prolegomena, p. 5)
dam pronatareto	(haplography).

16 MITIS: editors have felt uneasy about this word. Most fish are brutally savage (cf. Oppian 2.43 *et sq.*), thus the *scari* may be termed 'gentle' or 'kindly' (by a fairly usual 'inverse litotes' from *inmitis*) and Lenz (*Sokrates* (NF 10) 76 (1922), p. 143) draws attention to the vocabulary used in the parallel passage (1.4) from Aelian: φιλεῖν . . . . . . πεφυκότες. For *mitis*, cf., e.g., *Octauia* 398, *iustitia* . . . *terris regebat mitis* . . ., *ibid.* 979, *urbe est nostra mitior Aulis*, etc. So *aliquis mitis scarus*, 'any gentle parrot-fish', but it is odd to emphasize that the second *scarus* is *mitis*, as presumably all *scari* are: our author may have overlooked this.

HUNC: for the late position, cf. *M* 3.513, and *M* 3.694.

17 ATQUE LITA: my reading in the next line makes it probable that this line ended with an adverb which modified *liber* . . . *resultat*. Heinsius has been influenced by the *atque ita* of B to read *atque ita tandem*: we must seek the truth in A (cf. Prolegomena, p. 6). I fancy that the original text may have had the rare *citatim* or *citate* (*citatim* may have been a vulgar word as it is used by the author of *Bell. Afr.* (80.4); cf. *ThLL* 3.1202.60, cf. also Sedgwick, p. 19), and that a fairly simple haplography has given our text; on *l* for *c*, cf. Ms. *coci*, v. 85. It seems that the corruption in the next line is purely palaeographic; one cannot read the verb of 'pulling' that the parallel accounts require without assuming that deliberate alteration has been made in v. 18. Pliny is, unfortunately, non-committal.

18 VBERRER UATO QUEM TEXIT Q: RESULTET (Ms.): as the *atque* in the previous verse links back with an indicative, it seems best to assume that here, as in other cases, the second *e* in *resultet* has arisen from confusion with *a* (cf. Prolegomena, p. 5). Heinsius has restored the rest of the line to read: *liber seruato quem texit ciue*. The tag *seruato ciue* is supported by the passage in Aelian (1.4) where the *anthiae* are compared to trusty fellow-soldiers,[1] for the award of the crown *ob ciuis seruatos* would naturally occur to a Roman poet (cf. also *T* 3.1.48). *liber* for *Vber* is the simplest reading palaeo-graphically (for a ligatured *li* could easily be taken for an uncial *V*;

---

[1] ἀφῆκαν ἐλεύθερον also should be noted (Aelian 1.4).

cf. v. 74 initial letter), but, as Birt remarks (p. 82), is not so satisfactory, because properly it should mean 'springs back free' rather
than 'the free *scarus* springs back'. Schenkl's *uindex* (cf. τιμωροί in
Aelian) is more attractive, but, as the rest of the restoration admits
of a simple palaeographic explanation, I should doubtfully choose
liber (*ciue* gave *q:* through an intermediary *que*—for ligatured *ci*
and resemblance to *q*, cf. Steffens, pl. 22, line 13).

traxit, also suggested by Heinsius, is very attractive, but it is
difficult to see why so simple and appropriate a word should have
been changed to *texit*. The use of both *seruare* and *tegere* was, perhaps, like *oro atque obsecro*, a turn of Latin idiom: cf. Caesar, *ciu.*
1.85.2, *quos . . . conseruarit et texerit.*

The line as reconstituted is rather awkward, for it gives the main
point only by implication (viz. that the captured fish has been
rescued). As our author affects brevity (e.g. vv. 38-9), it seems
reasonable to accept the text adopted rather than attempt more
ambitious conjectures which cannot be defended from our short
text, and have next to no palaeographic probability. If we knew
more about our author's usage we could act more resolutely.

19 TARDA FUGAE: the use of a genitive to limit an adjective is a
not uncommon use in the poets,[1] e.g. *celer nandi*, 'swift in swimming',
Silius 4.585, but the only example with *tardus* known to the dic-
tionaries (and to Haustein, p. 74) shows a marked resemblance to
our passage: Val. Flacc. 3.547, *ille* [*ceruus*] . . . *tardusque fugae,
longumque resistens, sollicitat, suadetque pari contendere cursu*—'slow to
flee', and so it is to be understood here, for the closely related
squids are 'over short distances, the fastest moving creatures in the
sea'. Cf. an interesting article in the *Observer* (London), 25 Nov.
1956, by C. M. Yonge, who relates: 'The sequence of events . . . is
first a darkening almost to blackness, then, through the funnel, a
discharge of ink which forms a cloud of much the same size as the
animal. The same jet causes the squid to dart away, and simul-
taneously it turns as pale as it was dark before. The onlooker, or the
enemy, is left grasping at the dark shape which is cloud while, by
instantaneous change in place and in colour, the substance eludes
them.'

TENUI . . . UNDA: cf. Housman, *CR* 48 (1934), p. 139 (footnote):
'Reviewing Mr. Butler's earlier edition in C.R. 1905, p. 317, I
ought not to have blamed him for rendering [Prop.] I.11.11
"*tenui* unda" as "shallow", a sense established for instance by
Ouid. *met.* VIII, 559, and Quint. *inst.* XII.2.11; though the sense

---

[1] Cf. Erdmann, p. 2; Platnauer, *G&R* 13 (1944), p. 70; Brenous, p. 121 *et sq.*

found in Verg. *g.* IV.410, Ouid. *met.* VI.351, Manil. I.161 is equally appropriate.' The latter meaning seems to be 'thin, unsubstantial, tenuous'. Cf. *tenui sanguine, inf.* v. 123, and *tenuis . . . aqua* ('shallow') Liv. 1.4.6. The singular is used as in *M* 8.857, *piscis in unda.*

20 DEPRENSA EST: on a comparison with *utque sub aequoribus deprensum polypus hostem continet* (*M* 4.366) it might seem that we should take this verb to mean 'is caught'. Cf. also *M* 1.296, *hic summa piscem deprendit in ulmo.* Yet if the *sepia* is caught what use is the emission of ink? Consequently we should assume that the verb here means 'is discovered'. Cf. *M* 11.772, *lacu deprensa relicto accipitrem fluuialis anas* [*fugit*]. Plutarch does not help with 978AB, ὅταν καταλαμβάνηται, for this verb too has both meanings, cf. Thuc. 6.64.1 and Xen. *Mem.* 3.11.2. So, in English familiar use, 'caught' may mean 'discovered'.

IAMIAMQUE: as Müller, *de re metrica*[2], p. 276, remarks, if one were to write *iam iamque* here, the result would be a very harsh asyndeton. One should also note that according to *ThLL* (7.119.16 *et sq.*) *iamiamque* (or *iam iamque*) is used of that which is about to occur, whereas *iamiam* is a reduplicated *iam.* Now if Müller's observation is just, we have here *iamiam* connected to the previous sentence with *que,* so, according to the *ThLL,*[1] the meaning should be simply an emphatic *iam.* I am of opinion, however, that the text means 'just about to', as in *M* 12.588, *has iamiam casuras adspicis arces?* (where the idea of *iamiam* is clearly future) and *Aen.* 2.530, *sequitur, iamiam-que manu tenet.* It would seem that there is a certain hypallage and that the author meant *timetque manus iamiam rapacis,* for I do not see why the statement that the *sepia* was 'just about to fear' or 'just now fearing' the hunter, should be made. It makes much better sense to say that the *sepia,* slow to flee, is detected in the waters and fears the hunter who is about to catch it at any moment.

MANUS may be used with some general notion like 'power, violence', cf. Livy 21.41.16, *reputet nostras nunc intueri manus senatum populumque Romanum* (cf. also *ThLL* 8.354.54), for the bite of the *sepia* was dangerous (Oppian 2.455; Aelian 5.44), and hence the fisherman would hardly catch it with his hands. But probably our author is merely echoing *F* 4.706, *urentes effugit illa manus.*

RAPACIS I take with *manus* to mean 'plundering violence'. How is the *sepia* being hunted in our account? Hardly with weels or decoys (cf. *DT* 233), but rather with the trident. The parallel accounts

---

[1] But *ThLL* does not seem to distinguish *iamiam + que* from *iam iamque*: e.g. *Aen.* 2.530 (quoted above) (7.120.5) and *Aen.* 8.708, *et laxos iam iamque inmittere funes* (7.120.7).

are even more general than our text, for they merely talk of what
the *sepia* does when in terror. For the accusative plural in *is* one
should compare *minacis* (v. 45); *sequentis* (v. 22) and *omnis* (v. 81)[1]
are doubtful.

ILLA: Birt (p. 72) proposes to read *hilla* here and thus rid the text
of an objectionable repetition of *illa* in the next line. He shows that
the ancients[2] considered animals knew why they were being hunted;
that the *sepia* was hunted for the ink in its gland; that the gland was
called μήκων or μύτις by the Greeks, and that these words could
well be translated by *hilla*. When he goes on to claim that the singular
hilla is used because the *sepia* has no *uiscera* in the proper sense,
we are on less sure ground, and his case is further weakened by the
fact that the only attestations for the singular are in Varro, *ling.*
5.111 (where it is a grammarian's form, but not necessarily in use),
and in Laberius, v. 22 (*sensus obscaenus*) and v. 145.[3] The crucial
difficulty, to my mind, is the making of *hilla* the subject of the verb
timet. This seems extraordinary (indeed *hilla* would go better with
uomit), and must deter us from accepting Birt's ingenious conjecture.
(Sedlmayer in *WSt* 2 (1880), p. 293 *et sq.*, shows that Ovid avoided
closing two consecutive verses with the same word in the Metamorphoses, although there are words often repeated at the end of
pentameters[4] and occasionally hexameters in the other poems.)
Each *illa* in our text seems to be an imitation: *manus timet illa rapacis*
(v. 20) echoes *urentes effugit illa manus* (*F* 4.706), and *uomit illa cruorem*
(v. 21) echoes *uomit ille cruorem* (*M* 5.83).

21 NIGRUM: this word is used of the fluid of the nearly related
lolligo in v. 131, *inf.*

UOMIT ILLA CRUOREM: this restoration seems to be inevitable
when one adverts to the tag *uomit ille cruorem* (*M* 5.83; cf. *Aen.*
10.349, *Geo.* 3.516) and the use of ἴχωρ in Oppian. Cf. also ἀνήμεσαν,
Opp. 3.161. The *ore cruore* which Achilles Statius suggested is
impossible, because the *sepia* did not emit the ink from its mouth:
cf. Ar. 678 b 37.

22 AUERTITQUE UIAS: cf. the common phrase *auertere iter*
(Caes. *gall.* 1.23.1, etc.) and *auersum . . . Mycenis . . . iter* (Stat.
Theb. 1.683). From a comparison with Athen. 323 e we may assume
that the normal meaning of 'deflects her course' is meant: διωκομένη

---

[1] Cf. Commentary.
[2] E.g. Pliny, 8.7.
[3] For a proposal by Müller to read *hilla* in Lucilius, cf. Bücheler, *ALL* 3 (1886),
p. 144; cf. also Vollmer on *Priap.* 68.18 (*PLM* 2.ii (Leipzig, 1923)).
[4] The reasons are discussed by Axelson in 'Der Mechanismus des ovidischen
Pentameterschlusses' in *Ovidiana*, p. 121 *et sq.*

4—H.

τε ἡ σηπία τὸν θολὸν ἀφίησι καὶ ἐν αὐτῷ κρύπτεται ἐμφήνασα φεύγειν εἰς τοὔμπροσθεν. (Cf. Plutarch 978Β quoted a few lines below.) This interpretation rather tells against taking *tarda fugae* as 'slow to flee', for the implication here is that the *sepia* is on the move, and changes direction.

UIAS: evidently a 'poetic plural', but neither Maas nor Bednara remarks it.

OCULOS FRUSTRATA SEQUENTIS: cf. Plutarch 978Β, ὑπεκδῦναι καὶ ἀποδρᾶναι τὴν τοῦ θηρεύοντος ὄψιν, whence it seems that we should take *sequentis* as a genitive singular. This seems simpler than reading it as a plural with *oculos*, and may be paralleled by the similar use as a noun (*sequenti*), v. 63.

23 CLAUSUS RETE: obviously a seine-net is meant. *clausus* means that the escape of the *lupus* is cut off, but it is clear that he can still course about in the enclosed waters. Cf. Auson. *Mos.* 331, *clausos consaepto gurgite pisces*. . . .

INMITIS ET ACER: contrast *mitis*, v. 16. The ferocity of the *lupus* was notorious. *acer*: 'fierce', so *genus acre leonum*, Lucr. 5.862.

24 DIMOTIS CAUDA . . . ARENIS: cf. *dimotis impulsu pectoris undis*, *M* 4.708. Hence I take the phrase together.

ARENIS: the plural, where a singular was preferred by Caesar (*De Analogia* I: Funaioli, fr. 3a), is formally a 'poetic plural'; but (cf. Funaioli *ad loc.*) the arguments in favour of the plural (Gellius 19.8.7) may date from the time of Caesar.

SUBMISSUS: I take this as being in contrast with *inmitis et acer*: 'with downcast appearance, humble' (found in Vergil, *Aen.* 10.611 (cf. *Aen.* 3.93); but not in Ovid who uses *submissā voce*, and *submissā terrā* (having cast yourself on the ground) *EP* 3.1.149). It seems most improbable that it could be '*se submissus*' (cf. *bos . . . latus submisit in herba* (*M* 3.23)) 'having laid himself down'. Vollmer's *subnisus* seems unlikely; Plutarch's ἐνέωσεν (977F) would suggest it, but, according to Neue-Wagener iii.564, Livy is the only author in whom '*subnisus*' (*vice* '*subnixus*') is satisfactorily attested.

SIDIT: for *considit*. (*sidit* in Ovid only as *v.l.* at *M* 1.307.)

26 SALTU: Birt (pp. 74–5) proposed to read *astu* here on the ground that the *lupus*, if it lies on the bottom of the sea until the net passes over it, cannot be said to deceive the nets with a leap. Gesner solved the problem by filling in the gap with a reference to the *mugil*, a fish which does jump over the net. Cf. Oppian 3.98 *et sq.* This is an attractive solution of the difficulty at first sight, but as Pliny does not mention the *mugil* here (but cf. Plin. 9.32) it does not seem that our text is likely to have had an account parallel to

Oppian 3.98. Cassiodorus (*uar.* 11. 40. 7) when he says *alacer in undas exilit* seems to have our text in mind. It is very unlikely that he read our text in its mutilated form and conjectured what the interval should contain. Nor does Birt's proposal to read *astu* explain the awkward *emicat in auras*, for to add *atque dolos astu deludit inultus* seems to be rather an anticlimax, even though the chief idea may lie in *inultus*. Now, as *inultus* seems to read better with *deludit* in the sense of 'mocks' (rather than 'deceives')[1] it would accordingly seem that *saltu* reads better than *astu*. Then we must assume that there is a contrast with the previous mock humility of the *lupus*, and that the fish does in fact leap from the water.

For *deludo* in the sense of *ludo*, cf. Seneca, *Herc. O.* 944, *meamque fallax unda deludat sitim* (in most cases I am unable to be sure whether 'mock' or 'deceive' is intended: Verg. *Aen.* 6.344, 10.641, etc.). Yet the parallel *eludit* in v. 32 has the sense of 'avoided', and so the *ThLL* takes the verb *deludit* here. It may be noted that the next example the *ThLL* can offer in this sense with an impersonal object[2] is from Lact. *inst.* 5.17.33 [*animalia*] *insidias aliorum uario genere deludunt* (*ThLL* 5.473).

Prince Bonaparte (in the *Iconografia della fauna Italica*, vol. 3, Rome, 1841 (ref. 87)) agrees with this interpretation but adds significantly '[in Plinio] vedrá chiaramente detto, ma non bene osservato fin ora'. So de Saint-Denis, who has watched the *lupus* lie in his trench to let the net pass over, has nothing to say about any leap into the air (*Vocabulaire*, p. 61). O. Skutsch suggests that there has been some influence from the second anecdote related about the *lupus* (Oppian 3.129) where the *lupus* is described as ὑψόσ' ἀναθρώσκων.

27 ET: Birt suggests *at*. Both the previous anecdote and this one recount how a normally fierce fish escapes by means of cunning, so we may retain *et* since, it seems, no contrast is intended.

SIBI CONSCIA TERGI: I have not been able to find a satisfactory parallel[3] for this use of *sibi conscius* with a physical, and morally neutral, quality. I do not see that any moral quality can be read into the text, unless one may argue that *nocet* in v. 30 has some such idea. (Baehrens' conjecture at Val. Flacc. 5.3, *extremi sibi dudum conscius aeui*, has no moral force either—I believe it is false.)

28 AD: cf. Appendix 2.

LAXATA MAGIS: cf. *fidens magis*, v. 55, *inf.*   *laxiora* would be un-metrical.

---

[1] *et mecum lusos ridet inulta deos*, A 3.3.20.

[2] For personal object, cf. Avian. *fab.* 42.1, *lupum melior cursu deluserat haedus*, where this verb is required by the metre, just as in our text.

[3] Pliny (32.12) repeats the expression, but without *sibi* (cf. English 'conscious' and 'self-conscious').

CONIXA: the Ms. is corrupt and this reading of Schenkl's[1] gives excellent sense and may be supported by the word ὁρμηθεῖσαι ʼin Oppian (3.119). Haupt's *conuexa*, although he ingeniously argues in favour of it (p. xix) as an alternative form of *conuecta*, seems to be rather a colourless word. Sannazaro's *conuersa* is not impossible and recalls the δινεύονται of Oppian. Yet it is palaeographically unlikely. It seems best to take *conitor* as 'pushing its way to', cf. Liv. 42.65.8, *in tumulum conitebantur* (cf. Appendix 2).

29 PER MULTOS ... FLEXUS: 'with many a turn', cf. Appendix 2; *uiae flexus*, Liv. 29.34.9; and Manil. 1.440, *cui iuncta feruntur flexa per ingentis stellarum flumina gyros*; 1.570, *tarda . . . . . . per longos circumfert lumina flexus* [*Sol*].

30 ITER: for the use of *iter* as *uia*, cf. Caes. *gall.* 1.6.1, *erant omnino itinera duo. . . .*

31 AT CONTRA: again in our text at v. 118; cf. Appendix 1. The contrast thus emphasized is hardly that between the *arenis* in v. 24 and *scopulis* here, but rather the distinction between the active *murenae* and the sluggish *polypi*.

CRINALI: 'full of tentacles'; cf. Pliny 9.92, *conchas complexu crinium frangunt* [*polypi*]. *crinalis* is not indexed in Leumann's *Die lateinischen Adjektiva auf* -*lis* (Strassburg, 1917), but it is analogous to the examples he gives on pp. 30–1 of such adjectives derived from 'Körperteilnamen'. Such words usually mean 'pertaining to the portion of the body named' and are most often applied to garments: *talaris tunica* of a garment which reaches to the ankles (*talaria* (*M* 10.591)), *genualia, collare, cubital*, etc., and *crinale* (*M* 5.53; *EP* 3.3.15). This is the meaning that *crinalis* has in Vergil and Ovid, for it is used in the phrase *uitta crinalis* (three times in Ovid, cf. Verg. *Aen.* 7.403) and means *quae crinibus geritur*. Here the meaning is 'having many tentacles' or 'made of tentacles'. Leumann (p. 33) remarks on extensions of the proper use of the adjectives in this termination to such uses as *cornua lunaria*, crescent-shaped horns (*M* 9.688); *trabale telum*, a weapon as large as a beam (Vergil); *molares* (*saxa molaria*), rocks as big as mill stones (Vergil). Thus the use in our text seems a permissible but unique (*ThLL* 4.1201.30) poetic use of *crinalis*. (Leumann, *MH* 1 (1944), p. 147, may also be consulted; on p. 145 he shows that *crinitus* is the form which is normally used in such a context as ours.) We may suspect that the adjective here has been influenced by a Greek model, for the *ThLL*

---

[1] Cf. K. Schenkl, *Ph* 22 (1865), p. 540: '. . . ist das verderbte *connextat* ohne Bedenken in *connixa* umzuändern was in Handschriften nicht selten mit *connexa* verwechselt wird . . . *connixa* ist hier der passende Ausdruck' (as the *murena* has to press and wriggle through with difficulty).

(4.1205.40) gives an interesting example from the Glossaries: εὐπλόκαμος. πεπυκασμένος· comatus seu pulipus, crinitior, crine prolixior. Birt quotes Athenaeus 135 c, σηπίη εὐπλόκαμος, from Matron (cf. Hemsterhuys ad Lucian. dial. marin. 4.3). For the etymology of crinis and its restriction 'to the long hair of women and horses', cf. Dewitt, Language 16 (1940), p. 90.

SEGNIS: cf. Schmid: 'Halten sie sich auf felsigen Grunde auf . . .; über Tag bewegen sie sich wenig und sitzen stunden- und tagelang auf einem Flecke' (from O. Schmid, p. 262, 269), 'daher segnis' (p. 269).

32   PŌLYPUS: this word, from Plautus and Ennius onward, has a long o. As echenais, v. 99, inf., is a Doric form, it seems best to regard pōlypus as a transliteration of the Doric πώλυπος. Marx, however, on Plaut. Rud. 1010, suggests it may represent the Attic πουλύπους (used in Comedy, Athen. 318 f), just as Polydamas (Ep. 5.94; Persius 1.4; Prop. 3.1.29) represents Πουλυδάμας.

HAERET: scopulis haerere, M 3.592, 'to remain on the rocks', cf. pectoribus nostris haeretis amici (T 3.4b.17).

ELUDIT: cf. deludit, v. 26, but here this word clearly means 'to evade', cf. Manilius 5.163, cito motu rigidos eludere caestus.

HAC . . . FRAUDE: many editors have taken this to refer to the change of colour which follows, yet it seems unlikely that the octopus could be said to avoid nets by changing his colour; but by clinging to a rock he could evade the net which would pass over him if he clung so strongly that the weights could not move him. crinali corpore scopulis haeret, of course, go together, and emphasize the contrast with other fishes which have no method of grasping the rocks. It should be noted, however, that the author in vv. 86–7 points out that rocky portions of the sea-bed should be fished with lines, not with nets which suit the sandy bottom of the sea. Hence it seems that we should take hac in a retrospective sense here. If we do so, we shall be spared the difficulty of explaining et in the next line, for a subordinating conjunction would be required[1] if we were to take hac in a prospective sense.

33   ET: defended in preceding paragraph, but it is a very awkward connexion.

SUB: evidently means 'in accordance with, subject to'; but cf. Appendix 2.

LEGE LOCI: this phrase, without the preceding sub, is an Ovidian tag—AA 1.142; A 3.2.20, haec in lege loci commoda circus habet.

---

[1] It is, of course, for this reason that Hemsterhuys, ad Lucian. dial. marin. 4.3, suggested that ut with the subjunctive should be read for et with the indicative. (Cf. Plaut. Bacch. 35, quid si hoc potis est: ut tu taceas, ego loquar?)

34   EI: this form is found in the early dramatists, and Lucretius has nine examples (Axelson, *Unpoetische Wörter*, p. 70, where it is pointed out that in later poetry there was a tendency to avoid all forms of the pronoun *is*, *ea*, *id*, and that, of all the singular forms, *ei* is the rarest). Catullus 82.3 also has *ei*. The next examples in verse are in Germanicus, where curiously enough they have the same place in the line as our occurrence—*talis ei*, v. 333; *lactis ei*, v. 457.

Maurenbrecher (pp. 24–5) claims that none of the poets whose names are set out below have *ei*, although those whose names I italicize fairly frequently use other forms of the pronoun: *Cicero* (Aratea), *Vergil*, *Horace*, *Tibullus*, *Propertius*, *Ovid*, *Valerius Flaccus*, *Silius*, *Statius*, *Avienus*, *Ausonius* (two examples in prose), Lucan, Columella (verse), Persius, Petronius (verse), Martial, Juvenal, Dracontius, Phaedrus, Seneca (verse). Axelson claims that Lucretius has uniformly the spondaic scansion, and Lindsay (*Early Latin Verse* (Oxford, 1922), p. 168) rejects the iambic examples attributed to Plautus. (The references given by Lenz to Lachmann (*Kleinere Schriften* 2.98), and Jachmann (*Ph* 90 (1935), p. 336) are interesting. These articles also discuss the avoidance by the poets of *is qui* in the various cases. This seems, however, to be subordinate to the interest attaching to the use of the dative singular of *is* at all.)

PRAEDAM: cf. Pliny *nat.* 9.180, *suspecta fraus praedae* [i.e. *escae*] *est*. The word is more understandable in the case of the hunt, e.g. *M* 3.225, *ea turba* [i.e. *canes*] *cupidine praedae* [i.e. *Actaeonis*] ... *sequuntur*. *praedaret* of the Ms. must be due to the influence of *ubi* coupled with misunderstanding of the metaphor here (*ubi*: cf. Stolz-Schmalz, p. 767, 'auch in klass. Zeit ist zeitliches *ubi* nicht selten').

35   PENDENTEM SAETIS AUIDUS RAPIT: this may be translated as 'he greedily snatches the hanging (bait) with his tentacles', or 'he greedily snatches the (bait) which hangs on the line'. The first interpretation would seem to be favoured by Pliny's (32.12) *brachiisque complecti*, by the similar phrase in v. 38 (*cauda pendentem euerberat escam*), by the use of *crinalis*[1] in v. 31 for the tentacles, and by the account given in Oppian 4.300 *et sq.* of how the *polypus* was caught by means of a leafy branch garnished with hooks and towed through the water (Mair, *ad loc.*, quotes Apostolides to show that a similar method is still used in Greece), so that no question of a line would enter into the fishing. In this regard the use of the plural *hamos*[2] by Pliny, and the fact that he does not mention any line

---

[1] Cf. τρίχες, σπεῖραι in Greek (Hemsterhuys, *loc. cit.*).
[2] But cf. Opp. 3.470, for one line and many hooks.

would make one interpret him as envisaging the method mentioned in Oppian; yet he talks of *harundine leuatum extra aquam*, which seems clearly to indicate angling.

In favour of the second interpretation may be urged the passage in Plutarch setting out the use of horses' hair for making lines (977A), ἱππείαις γὰρ θριξὶ χρῶνται (cf. Opp. 3.469), and the frequent use of *saeta* for the fisherman's line: *saeta . . . quaerit in mari praedam*, Mart. 10.30.16, *piscem tremula salientem ducere saeta*, Mart. 1.55.9. The use of the plural of *saeta* in our text can be explained as being due to metrical necessity, but two hairs are recommended by Cotton[1] (cf. *lina secat*, v. 48).

As the *polypus* is caught on the line (cf. an interesting article— lamentably 'popular' in tone—in *Frontiers* (Philadelphia) 19 (1955), p. 99), and as Pliny has *harundine* (for the Greek *calamo* in our text; cf. v. 87). I am satisfied that we must take the reference to angling as being what is meant here. Finally, and most conclusively, that angling must be meant here is shown by the arrangement of method of capture that is illustrated in the table I set out:

1. *Scarus* (v. 9), weel
    (a) self freeing
    (b) fellow freeing
2. *Sepia* (v. 19), ?trident
3. *Lupus* (v. 23), net
4. *Murena* (v. 27), net

5. *Polypus* (v. 31)
    (a) clings to rocks, net
    (b) changes colour
    (c) gnaws bait, hook
6. *Mugil* (v. 38), hook
7. *Lupus* (v. 39), hook
8. *Murena* (v. 43), hook
9. *Anthias* (v. 46), hook

HIC QUOQUE FALLIT: *sic quoque fallebat*, M 1.698. *hic quoque*: 'in this matter, too', i.e. when sought by the angler, in contrast to the previous method of catch.

36 ELATO CALAMO would seem to be 'ablative absolute', but might be taken as instrumental, if *emersus* is taken as passive. Even a modern angler using a reel raises his rod to 'strike' a biting fish.

CUM DEMUM: this is a very unusual type of phrase. The usual constructions are of the form: *tum demum . . . cum . . .* and *ita demum . . . ut. . . .* There seems to be no other example of this con-struction, and the *ThLL* (5.518.30) places this under '*III uaria et singularia. . . .* B. i. q. *denique, postremo, . . .* de ordine rerum tem-poruмue ipso', and quotes examples where *demum* is an independent[2] word: Lucr. 1.486; Ovid, *M* 15.122 (Heinsius and others emend

---

[1] Walton and Cotton, *The Compleat Angler*, part 2, cap. 5.
[2] i.e. not attached to a conjunction.

this passage); Sen. *Herc. F.* 242. The remaining passage—Suet. *Cal.*
6.2, *et ut demum fato functum palam factum est*—shows the same phenomenon that we have here—*demum* is in the unemphatic introductory
clause. It may be possible to presume that we should read the
common *tum demum*, with a colon after *fallit*, understanding *hic
quoque fallit: elato calamo emersus in auras, tum demum brachia dissoluit.*
For confusion of *c* and *t*, cf. A's version of *soleae*, v. 124.

EMERSUS: the verb *emergere* is normally intransitive, but the past
participle is used in a middle sense, meaning 'having raised one's
self from the water'. It is possible so to take *emersus* here (although
perhaps not the most natural way to read the text (cf. Pliny (32.11):
leuatum)), and this seems preferable, as the *ThLL* (5(2).475.30, 64)
can quote only two cases of a passive usage of the past participle:
Mart. Cap. 9.921, and Amm. 19.8.11, and it admits that both
of these have a considerable element of doubt as to whether they
are really passive at all. The *ThLL* 5(2).473.40 indicates that
emergo is transitive at *Dirae* 57 (but an intransitive sense seems just
possible, with *corpora* as a nominative), and Cat. 64.14 (so Haupt,
Opusc. i.107, believes, but Vahlen, in the Berlin *Sitzungsberichte* for
1905 (p. 761), argues strongly against Haupt).

37 BRACHIA DISSOLUIT: Birt castigates this expression, but if one
considers the image of the octopus with his tentacles twined in a
knot around the bait, then the expression is seen to fall into line with
the common *nodum, uincula soluere* (cf. Lucr. 6.356; Cic. *orator* 235.
facilius est apta dissoluere, quam dissipata conectere). The *ThLL* takes it
(5.1498.42) as *diducere, dispergere, diffundere* and compares Vitruv.
2.8.1[1] ([*genus structurae*] *reticulatum ad rimas faciendas ideo paratum
quod in omnes partes dissoluta habet cubilia et coagmenta*) which seems
very unlike this use.

BRACHIA: the tentacles of the octopus, cf. Pliny 9.85, [*polypi*] *per
brachia uelut acetabulis dispersis haustu quodam adhaerescunt.*[2]

POPULATUM: Ovid uses *populari* with objects *capillos* (*M* 2.319) and
formam (*MF* 45): one can hardly object to it here.

38 MUGIL: for the anecdote which follows, cf. parallels quoted
by Lenz, and Aristotle 591 a 19.

PENDENTEM: cf. v. 35.

EUERBERAT: compare μαστίζω in Oppian 3.521. At *Aen.*
12.866 this verb means, I think, simply 'strikes'. Ovid's only use at
M 14.577 imitates *Aen.* 12.866, but, at *M* 14.577 and here, the
preposition seems to convey the idea of *excutere*.

---

[1] And some uses from the Vulgate.
[2] *ThLL* approves form *bracchia*—2,2156.58.

ESCAM (cf. v. 11): for the meaning 'bait', cf. Plaut. *Asin.* 221, *auceps sum ego: esca est meretrix*; Plin. *nat.* 10.194, etc. *at* perhaps marks the contrast of the *mugil* which will not take the bait, as distinct from the *polypus* which will not let it go.

39 LEGIT: implies no such notion as in Horace, *sat.* 1.3.117, *et qui nocturnus sacra diuum legerit*, with an implication of theft (an analysis of *sacrilegus*). Compare Plutarch 977B, ἀνακάπτων (cf. Herodotus 2.93.2, where it is also used of fish, and no such notion could be present).

Rohde (p. 17) has a useful observation that Ovid began new items on new lines, but it seems imprudent to urge this as an argument against Ovidian authorship in so short a passage as that about the *lupus*.

LUPUS: cf. v. 23, and v. 112.

ACRI CONCITUS IRA: Vlitius and Birt have tried to emend the text here by reading *aere* (i.e. *hamo*)[1] and some support is to be found for this view in the parallel passages in Pliny, Oppian, and Plutarch, all of which describe the hooking of the fish. In view of the extreme brevity of our poet (the previous sentence is a good example), I have no doubt that he was satisfied to have the reader infer from *hamus*, v. 42, that angling was in question. In the previous sentence the parallel accounts also mention the hook, but our author has no reference to it other than *pendentem*. Furthermore the use of *acer* in the sense of physical sharpness is not very usual in the poets[2] while the metaphorical sense is very common (e.g. of this very fish, v. 23); for *acris ira*, cf. Lucretius 3.311, 6.753, and, for the whole phrase, cf. *rabida qui concitus ira* (*M* 7.413) and *ira tum percitus acri*, Lucr. 5.399.

40 FERTUR: the passive of *ferre* seems here, as often, to denote a rushing motion over which the subject has no deliberate control: Verg. *Aen.* 8.548, *pars cetera prona fertur aqua . . .*; *AA* 3.667, *quo feror insanus?*; Ovid, *Frg.* 2, *feror huc illuc, uae, plena deo*. For the whole phrase, cf. *concita cursu fertur*, F 4.462. We must assume that the poet's wish is to describe an instinctive reaction on the part of the fish.

For this use of the singular of *uarius*, cf. *terre uaria formidine ceruos*, *RA* 203, and for the use in respect of direction, cf. *uariarum ambage uiarum*, *M* 8.161. Cf. notes on *uarie*, v. 89, *inf.*

FLUCTUSQUE FERENTES PROSEQUITUR (Ms.): this is a most difficult phrase. The parallel passages do not help. The repetition of *ferentes*—

---

[1] Cf. *EP* 2.7.10, [*piscis*] . . . *omnibus unca cibis aera subesse putat,*
[2] Cf. *ThLL* 1.357.24.

fertur and the meaning of *prosequitur* are the features that cause the most trouble. *prosequitur* is literally 'to follow forth', but, of course, has a wide range of derived meanings, of which, perhaps, that of 'accompanying' is the most common and is suggested by Vergil's *prosequitur . . . uentus euntis* (*Aen.* 3.130) used of a favourable wind. Now the only reason the fish should 'accompany' the waves is surely to gain momentum so that he can pit his strength against the hook and line. If this is the case it is not necessarily incompatible with *discursu uario*, as the fish could proceed[1] in a form of 'tacking' (cf. Brehm quoted by Schmid, p. 265, 'Schwimmt mit erstaunlicher Kraft hin und her') in the general direction of the waves. What is difficult is to see how the fish can be said to 'follow' the waves which 'bear' him (*ferentes*). In Lucan 5.419, the Mss. vary between *furens* (*flatus*) and *ferens* (*flatus*), where *furens* gives the better sense. I do not see that *furentes* or *frementes* (cf. Verg. *Geo.* 2.160) will improve matters in our text.

I have been convinced that the reading proposed tentatively by O. Skutsch ought to be accepted: *fluctusque furentem prosequitur*, 'and a wave attends him as he rages'. This involves a very abrupt change of subject, and the words must be taken in a parenthesis like *dominumque uocando increpitant* (vv. 79-80), which takes the same position in the line as our phrase. The meaning of *prosequitur* is then neatly paralleled by the passage from Vergil quoted already (*prosequitur . . . uentus=fluctus . . . prosequitur*), and all trouble about *ferentes* is avoided.

41 UULNERE . . . LAXATO: possibly an 'ablative absolute', but cf. Appendix 2. It seems rash to follow Vollmer in restoring such forms as *uolnere*, as our Ms. does not show them in the *Halieutica*, although they are found in Grattius.

42 LAXATO: for this verb, cf. *laxans* (v. 14), and *laxant arua sinus*, *Geo.* 2.331.

SAEUUS . . . HAMUS: the fact that there is no particular force in the placing of *saeuus* between *laxato* and *uulnere* will naturally make one cautious about arguments from order elsewhere, e.g. *sidit*, v. 24, *segnis*, v. 31.

ORA: poetic plural.[2]

43 NEC . . . UIRES NESCIT: cf. *uires nouerat ille suas*, *Ep.* 13.56; *uim spinae nouitque suae*, v. 47, *inf.*; *nec enim nescit . . . M* 12.27; and *nouit torpedo uim suam*, Pliny 9.143. With this sentence the poet seems to recall the point that he stressed so strongly in the first ten verses—

---

[1] Cf. τῇ δεῦρο κἀκεῖ παραλλάξει, Plutarch 977B.
[2] Cf. Maas *ALL* 12 (1902), p. 541, and Bednara *ALL* 14 (1906), p. 560.

that the animals knew their innate powers—N.B. *proprias*: each
has his own.

44 From the paraphrase in Pliny 32.13 it is clear that our text
must have stated that the *murena* swallowed the hook and bit the
line: *murenae amplius deuorant quam hamum: admouent dentibus lineas*
atque ita erodunt. This implies that there is a lacuna in the text here.
The difficulty of suggesting a construction or emendation for
auxilioque sui indicates that the lacuna should follow these words.[1]
Then *nec comminus* may be taken to mean *ne comminus quidem* (cf.
Haupt-Korn-Ehwald on *M* 11.471), with a consequent implication
that the *murena* was also described as resisting *eminus* by biting the
line. This reconstruction substantially agrees with the account
given in the Armenian translation of the lost work of Philo Judaeus
entitled *Alexander, seu de Animalibus* in § 36:

Dicunt qui †Semelae† res narrauerunt, quod genus est marinum,
cooperationis daemonis cuiusdam usum; quod, si nequeat sub initio euitare
multiplicem hominum industriam malignam, postremum[2] eorum irrup-
tionem irritam reddit. Quippe quod hamum nulla exquisita esca obductum
uelut cibum inglutit: malum tamen effugiendi remedium inuenit; inuadens
enim et currens sursum, funiculum comedit; geminum emolumentum
ferens: et sibi salutem comparans, et punitionem in eum, qui manu
iniuriosus fuit. (Latin trans. by J. B. Aucher (Venice, 1822), p. 142.)

E. de Saint-Denis in his *Vocabulaire* ... (p. 71) discusses how the
murena fights savagely even when captured (cf. *captiua*, v. 45).
Cf. also *Ovidiana*, pp. 447-8, and add to the passages cited there,
Lucian, *dial. mort.* 8.

Vlitius, who first advanced the theory of a lacuna, restored the
text to read:

> *auxilioque sui ⟨dentis stridentia furtim*
> *fila cibosque rapit;⟩ morsu nec comminus acri....*

MORSU ... ACRI: cf. *acris ... morsus*, Cat. 2.4.

45 DEFICIT: perhaps 'grow weary of', cf. Seneca *Ep.* 51.10,
deficit puluere ille unctus et nitidus [*miles*]; from *ThLL* 5.327 it seems a

---

[1] Any suggestion to take *auxilio* and *morsu* as being in apposition seems impossible
—Velleius 2.45.1 is very slender evidence for a co-ordinate *que ... nec ...*, meaning *nec ... nec*, in Ovid's period (cf. Stolz-Schmalz, p. 663), for there the *neque*
supplemented by editors seems to be correct.

[2] I read *postremum*, presuming *postremam* is a misprint; and I have slightly
altered the spelling and punctuation.

preposition is required in the sense of *desistere*, but a poet might easily omit the preposition.

46 ANTHIAS: I hope to discuss the scansion of *anthias* elsewhere, but cf. Appendix 6.

HIS TERGO QUAE NON UIDET UTITUR ARMIS: it seems to be indisputable that the Ms. *his* is corrupt here. There are two serious difficulties:

(*a*) *his* agreeing with the noun *armis* and being antecedent to the relative clause. The two examples from Juvenal quoted by Owen: Juv. 6.532, *ergo hic ... meretur honorem ... qui ... currit derisor Anubis*; Juv. 7.41, *haec ... domus seruire iubetur, in qua sollicitas imitatur ianua portas*, and a further passage I have noted, *Rhet. Her.* 4.43.55, *quis est ... qui non hunc hominem ... laudet ... qui ... periculum ... suscipiat?* do not seem to be quite satisfactory as parallels, for the relative clause identifies one out of many (this is also the case in the archaic formula in Livy 22.10.2), but in our text a piece of description is added.[1] In Juv. 6.532 *Anubis* may be read in the relative clause.

(*b*) The lack of a preposition with *tergo* which is particularly harsh when *uidet* follows so closely. Ovid seems always to use either an adjective with the noun or a preposition, but cf. on *imo*, v. 90; Appendix 2; Birt, pp. 27-8.

Vollmer's conjecture, although plausible palaeographically, seems to be impossible Latin, as it comes either to *armis in tergo utitur*, or *armis, quae in tergo non uidet, utitur*. Heinsius' *tergi* seems to be palaeographically unlikely.

47 Although one might expect the *spina* to give some clue to the identity of the *anthias*, the fish is wrapped in impenetrable anonymity despite the fact that he is celebrated in Greek literature and often mentioned. It would seem that even in antiquity there was doubt on it, for Aristotle says (570 b 20) that 'some' call the *aulopias* the *anthias*, and Dorion (ap. Athen. 282 d) says that 'the anthias some also call *callichthys* and also *callionymos* and *elops*'. D'Arcy Thompson (pp. 14-15) suggests that two fish were meant: (1) *Anthias sacer* (Bloch) (*Serranus anthias, CV.*) (*le Barbier*), a small fish with a razor-like spine in the dorsal fin which would certainly suit the little we have in our text; and, because the account in Oppian (3.192) where it takes the Basse as bait implies it must be a large fish: (2) a large fish: ?the Great Sea Perch. As ancient accounts differed (Athenaeus discusses the problem at length, 282 c *et sq.*, and comes to no con-

---

[1] *hic* used as a simple definite article is very late, cf. Stolz-Schmalz, p. 482; *ThLL* 6.2737.72 *et sq.*

clusion), it would seem that all we can do is to admit the *anthias sacer* could well have had this tale told about him on account of his sharp spine. To compare accounts that are contradictory and try to make a firm identification of the fish mentioned here seems to be labour in vain.

Perhaps the fish was not found in Greek waters at all, and the tales about it came from the East, so that the doubts in ancient authors would be understandable. D'Arcy Thompson in the *Journal of Egyptian Archaeology* 14 (1928), p. 24, suggests an Egyptian fish, *Tilapia Nilotica*, which is called *ᵓan-it* in the hieroglyphics. One might also note the Red Sea fish *Acanthurus leucosternon* (or Surgeon-fish), which has 'a razor-edged lancet sheathed in a slot at the base of its tail. When in danger it erects the spine' with which it 'inflicts deep gashes' according to the *National Geographic Magazine* 109 (1956), p. 185.

QUE: for the postponement of this enclitic conjunction, cf. Appendix 1.

UERSO . . . CORPORE: cf. Sall. *Iug.* 107.1, *caecum corpus ad hostis uortere*, where *corpus* means *tergum*. As Vlitius indicates, *uerso corpore* is to be taken as 'ablative absolute', for it is the *spina* that does the cutting.

SUPINUS: 'on his back', cf. Pliny *nat.* 11.88, *[apes] noctu deprehensae in expeditione excubant supinae, ut alas a rore protegant.*

48 LINA: *linum* is the Ovidian word for a fishing line: cf. *M* 3.586, 13.923; *RA* 208. (For plural, cf. *saetis*, v. 35—neither Maas nor Bednara remarks it; *lina*, *M* 13.931, means 'nets'.)

FIXUM: cf. *M* 6.227, *medioque in pectore fixa tela gerit.*

INTERCIPIT: 'to cut off', cf. *M* 6.379.

49 CETERA: with this word we enter the second portion of the fragment, and we are faced with the task of elucidating the connexion with the first 48 lines. This is so difficult that Heinsius believed that Ovid's executor attempted to insert into the *Halieutica* a fragment which he had found in the poet's papers. Merkel commented 'uersus . . . plane aliunde petitos puto' and bracketed vv. 49-81. H. Fränkel has developed the theory still further and sees in the poem a hash of casual jottings left as a sketch by Ovid (p. 160; p. 252). The other view was held by Birt, who asked (p. 11) why, in a poem of some 800 lines, of which this is just a fragment, a digression of some 30 lines could not be admitted. Gesner, and Vollmer (*RhM* 55 (1900), p. 530), hold that the 'digression' is really a fundamental part of the exposition of the argument (Vollmer is so dogmatic as to claim 'extra . . . ullam dubitationem').

It does seem to be undeniable that in vv. 49-51 the author contrasts the natural instincts that impel the wild animals on land either to seek flight in cowardly terror or to attack their hunters with foolhardy courage, with the natural instincts of the fishes, which have been shown to avoid destruction by cunning wiles. This implies something like the contrast between hunting and fishing which is found in the introduction to Oppian's *Halieutica* (1.12 *et sq.*). In other respects there are similarities of plan in our *Halieutica* and Oppian's (cf. Birt, pp. 103, 106), so there must be a certain bias in our arguments in favour of the belief that our text has lost some lines making a contrast between hunting and fishing. Birt's remark (pp. 10–11) that *cetera* implies a contrast that could hardly find a place in a *Cynegetica* is to be noted, but such arguments from isolated words which may have been specially inserted to form a link, are not so conclusive as general inferences from the whole purpose of a passage. For the structure of the line, cf. *M* 1.416, *cetera diuersis tellus animalia formis . . . peperit.*

DENSAS . . . SILUAS: cf. *densis . . . siluis*, *M* 15.488. These words seem to imply that the *siluestria animalia* are contrasted with domesticated animals mentioned later as the hunter's helpers. The phrase may, however, be purely pictorial, so that no specific contrast is implied.

50 UANI . . . TIMORES: 'groundless fears', cf. *uano . . . timore*, *EP* 3.6.43.

QUATIUNT SEMPER are presumably to be taken together.

LYMPHATA: Birt (pp. 24–5) has a discussion on this word and objects to it on the ground that it means the animals are insane or panic-stricken, and says that the poet who claims the *animalia* are *semper lymphata*, when he has already discussed in vv. 7–9 how they are given natural instinct to fend for themselves, must be 'ipse lymphatus'. This sort of criticism is too harsh, for an examination of the passage shows that *semper* can be taken with *quatiunt* and *lymphata* understood proleptically: 'groundless fears always terrify them into panic', and *lymphata* here is of a piece with *non sana ferocia* in the next line. That nature has given some animals instincts for their self-preservation which occasionally cause them to behave in a completely senseless manner is a fact that is evident to all. If this interpretation of the text can stand, then it is not necessary to follow the arguments of Birt.

lymphata is used in *M* 11.3 of the Bacchic frenzy; it is also found in Horace, Vergil, Lucan, Silius, and Statius, as well as the prose writers.

51 TRAHIT IN PRAECEPS: cf. *rapit in praeceps*, *A* 2.9.29, and Verg. *Geo.* 1.203, where *trahit* is found in R. There is generally a notion of

hastening to destruction in such phrases, and the original idea of 'falling headlong from a height' is obscured.

Birt points out (p. 25) that *insana* would fit the metre here, and claims that the only excuse for using such equivalent forms as NON SANA was that of metrical necessity. His pupil W. Pfeiffer[1] when investigating this question came to the same conclusion, but his work does not examine the use of negatives in Ovid. It would seem desirable to go into the question further. Cf. *non sani* Prop. 1.1.26 (*metri gratia*).

FEROCIA is a rather rare word and is not found in the poets after Pacuvius and Accius. Seneca uses it in the dialogues, but not elsewhere. However, it is found more frequently in prose writers (cf. Pliny *nat.* 8.188, Tac. *Agr.* 37.6, etc.). Livy is fond of it: e.g. 42.9.1, *ferocia animi*, *ThLL* 6.565.6. In view of the continual use of animals to illustrate points by the poets its avoidance can hardly be accidental, particularly as it is convenient metrically. For *mens* used of animals, cf. *iniquae mentis asellus*, Hor. *sat.* 1.9.20. Owen's reference to Verg. *Geo.* 3.73 is inadequate support for *gentis*. Natural instinct must be considered as resting in the mind, although *mens* is predominantly the word for rational mind. In *Culex* 179, *ardet mente* [*serpens*] there is hardly any notion of reasoning.

52 IPSA SEQUI NATURA MONET UEL COMMINUS IRE: taken without the context this verse clearly means: 'Nature herself advises to follow or to come to close quarters.' Editors have been sorely perplexed to explain them. *sequi* is wholly unsuitable to describe anything in the lines following (vv. 53–65), as, although the foolhardy animals come to grips with the hunters, the hunters do not run, for they kill the animals. To say these animals follow them is nonsense. Similarly the timid animals do not follow, but are followed. Merkel and Schenkl clearly see the difficulty, but their conjectures cannot be taken seriously; Birt's *saepta* seems to be just as improbable. (Postgate's *illa* must mean *illa animalia*, and confusion with *ipsa* was very probable (cf. Housman, *JPh* 16 (1888), p. 23), but the fundamental difficulty still remains.)

Keydell (p. 423) evidently despaired of any emendation on the lines of his predecessors, and propounded the theory that the subject to *sequi* and *comminus ire* was *homines* or *uenatores* to be supplied by the reader. Apart from the intrinsic difficulty of supplying these words

---

[1] *Quibus legibus 'non' et 'haud' particulae apud poetas Romanos ... positae sint* (Diss. Marburg, 1908), pp. 19 *et sq.* Exceptions which occur are due to the fact that the forms are not really equivalent in meaning, e.g. *Aen.* 4.520, where *non aequa* could not be replaced by *iniqua*. Cf. English 'not comparable' and 'incomparable'.

(*uenantum*, v. 53, despite Keydell, is not sufficient defence), there is no clear way to explain why the poet should interject hunters here. If we read the passage without v. 52 all is clear—what conceivable point is there in dragging in the hunters?

Now, as will be seen in the next paragraph, *comminus ire* is a phrase often used of the hunt, and *sequi* is suitable to describe the activity of the chase. This makes one suspect that Keydell was on the track of the correct interpretation of the lines. Hence we see that the text reads well without v. 52, and that v. 52 is suitable to another context; when we consider that it is repeated in the Ms. (at 65a), and that it will be found to be essential for the understanding of the text in the second place (cf. notes on v. 65a), then all the evidence points to the theory that it is repeated here in error, and that we should reject it from the text (on such repetitions, cf. Clark, pp. 448–9, p. 132, etc.; Havet § 1487 (Lucan 1.37)).

To complete the argument above we may note that *comminus ire* is often used of hunting by the poets: e.g. Prop. 2.19.22, and *F* 5.176, *audet et hirsutas comminus ire leas.*

53 INPIGER: cf. Hor. *carm.* 4.3.4, *equŏs inpiger.*

LEO: we cannot assume the author has seen a lion hunt: the description could have been inspired by the Circus, but I believe that it is copied from Vergil as explained *infra*.

PERGIT: motion is implied here, cf. *infert* (54), *uenit* (55), *properat* (57)—the lion attacks the hunter. We can hardly take *sternere pergit* as little more than *sternit* in accordance with the Lucretian use remarked by Bailey in his edition of Lucretius, i.101, cf. v. 83, *inf.*

54 AGMINA: used of hunters, cf. Val. Flacc. 3.522, *respicit ac pulchro uenantes agmine nymphas.* The plural seems to be 'poetic', as often.

INFERT SUA PECTORA: *aduersum fidens fer pectus in hostem*, Verg. *Aen.* 11.370, would seem to be a line that has influenced our author, cf. *fidens* in v. 55. *infert* does not seem so good a word as the simple *fert*, in view of such phrases as *inferet arma tibi*, *RA* 246, but the allusion to carrying weapons may be deliberate. Cf. Verg. *Aen.* 12.540, *dedit obuia ferro pectora.*

PECTORA: poetic plural first found in Cic. *Arat.* 461 (Bednara, *ALL* 14 (1906), p. 560); used of animals *M* 4.690, etc.

55 QUOQUE UENIT FIDENS MAGIS ET SUBLATIOR ARDET, (CONCUS-SITQUE TOROS ET UIRIBUS ADDIDIT IRAM,): the cardinal point to be noted here is that *uenit* and *ardet* are present tenses, while *concussit* and *addidit* are perfects. Valuable clues to what the author meant will be found from two passages I set out:

(*a*) Verg. *Aen.* 12.4 *et sq.*,

> *Poenorum qualis in aruis*
> *saucius ille graui* uenantum *uulnere pectus*
> tum demum *mouet arma leo, gaudetque comantis*
> *excutiens ceruice* toros, fixumque *latronis*
> *impauidus frangit telum, et fremit ore cruento.*

(It is hard to resist the conclusion that our author has copied this; as well as the words in roman type, cf. *ille* in Vergil, and *ecce*, v. 53.)

(*b*) Lucan 1.205 *et sq.*,

> *sicut squalentibus aruis*
> *aestiferae Libyes, uiso leo comminus hoste*
> *subsedit dubius, totam dum* colligit iram:
> *mox, ubi se saeuae stimulauit* uerbere caudae
> *erexitque iubam, et uasto graue murmur hiatu*
> *infremuit, tum, torta leuis si lancea Mauri*
> *haereat, aut latum subeant uenabula pectus,*
> *per ferrum tanti securus uolneris exit.*

It is clear from these passages that the lion was believed first to work himself into a fury, and then advance on the attackers: hence, in our text, the events in v. 56 are prior to those in v. 55, and the sequence of tenses is thus explained.

Emil Baehrens has suggested that there must be a lacuna in the text which contained the *hoc* or *eo magis* that is required to correspond with the *quo . . . magis* in v. 55. This necessitates reading v. 56 as an explanatory parenthesis. I have adopted this suggestion rather than the view that I originally held.

SUBLATIOR: this is an unusual form, but, as Birt points out (p. 37), it does occur in Cic. *dom.* 95. It seems that metrical reasons have here prevented the poet from using the more normal *elatior*, cf. Donatus on Ter. *Hec.* 507, *sublati animi sunt:* '*noue pro* elatis sublatos *dixit. et hoc proprie ferarum est* (ut: attollitque animos)[1], *nam bestiae pro animi qualitate uel erigunt corpora uel deponunt.*'

ARDET: cf. *M* 5.166 [*tigris*] . . . *ruere ardet.*

56 CONCUSSITQUE TOROS: cf. Vergil's *gaudet . . . excutiens ceruice toros, Aen.* 12.7.

57 It is unfortunate that the first word here should be corrupt, and that the lacuna which precedes makes its certain restoration impossible. *Prima facie* we should expect a word to describe some activity prior and akin to the idea in the remainder of the line. Such are Sannazaro's *prosilit* and Gesner's *proruit*. It is difficult to see why these words should have given *prodedit. prodigus* (Vlitius) and *prodigi*

---

[1] Verg. *Aen.* 12.4; cf. also *animis elate superbis, ibid.* 11.715.

('sc. *uires*', Vollmer) are open to the same objection. Burman's *procidit* is more plausible palaeographically, but how the idea can fit into the context is hard to see. *procidit* is not a suitable word, for it is not by falling that the lion 'hastens his doom with his strength'. It seems hardly possible that the last line, which should contain the climax, did not drive home the notion that it was of his own free will and impelled by his *ferocia mentis* that the lion made his fatal charge.[1] (Gesner seems to desire to take *letum* as the object of *proruit*: 'Mallem *proruit* si actiue acciperetur', cf. Ter. *Eun.* 599, *simul omnes foras proruont se.* Rather strange, and hardly required.)

58 FOEDUS: 'ugly'; cf. Sall. *Cat.* 15.5, *foedi oculi.* There is often an implication of 'repulsive' in this word: *M* 10.319, *M* 8.155, etc. The beginning of the line is reminiscent of *foeda Lycaoniae*, *M* 1.165; *Ibis* 431.

LUCANIS: cf. Honigmann, *RE* 26.1543, 'Das waldreiche Gebirge [of Lucania] . . . war reich an wilden Tieren, *besonders Bären*' (Varro, *ling.* 5.100, Mart. *spect.* 8.1, Galen (Kühn) 6.666). The reference in Martial is to a bear in the amphitheatre. Keller in Sandys' *Companion to Latin Studies* (p. 48) seems to imply that the wild bear became rare in Italy after the time of Augustus. Ovid makes no mention of Lucania in his extant works.

PROUOLUITUR: this word seems a little odd here, as it is often used of suppliants falling at a victor's feet (e.g. Liv. 6.3.4). I believe the bear is said to 'roll forward' because our author has in mind the words *se rotat* used in Lucan 6.222 (quoted *infra* in Appendix 5). Cf. *Atti*, p. 38. When the bear is captured he rolls about in the net—Plutarch, *quaest. nat.* 919 A: this is hardly what is meant here.

ANTRIS: bears do lurk and hibernate in caves, so it seems unnecessary to insist that *antra* should be taken as *conualles*, as in Prop. 1.1.11 (cf. Housman on Manil. 5.311). The plural does not seem to be required but lends, perhaps, a poetic atmosphere.

59 QUID NISI PONDUS INERS, cf. *M* 1.6,

> *unus erat toto naturae uultus in orbe,*
> *quem dixere Chaos: rudis indigestaque moles*
> *nec quidquam nisi pondus iners congestaque eodem*
> *non bene iunctarum discordia semina rerum.*

INERS: 'inert' cannot be the meaning in our text, for the *ursus prouoluitur*, and so we must seek the primary significance (*ThLL*

---

[1] Cf. *Aen.* 9.551 *et sq.*,

> *ut fera quae densa uenantum saepta corona*
> *contra tela furit, seseque haud inscia morti*
> *inicit, et saltu supra uenabula fertur.*

7.1308.75), viz. *arte carens*, and see much the same idea as in *stolidus*. Cf. *inertis*, 'ineffectual', Verg. *Aen.* 10.322; *tempus* . . . *iners* ('wasted time') *AA* 3.60.

[FEROCIA MENTIS]: these words are corrupt and a lacuna must be marked in the text—cf. O. Skutsch, *Ovidiana*, p. 450: 'The existence of a lacuna is proved by three facts: (1) the genuine end of 59 is missing and has been replaced, in defiance of concord (*stolidi . . . mentis*), by the last two words of 51. (2) The destruction of the bear is not mentioned (contrast 57 and 62). (3) The bare participle *actus* with *aper* is awkward and colourless, and is shown to be a mere remnant by Virg. *Aen.* 10,707f. *ac uelut ille canum morsu de montibus altis/ actus aper*. If (3) were the only objection to the passage, it might mean no more than that the poet had been driven into an infelicity by taking over *actus aper* from Virgil. As it is, the two other objections prove that the poet imitated the whole cast of the Virgilian passage (as Statius, for instance, did, *Theb.* 8,532 *qualis saetigeram Lucana cuspide frontem/ strictus aper*), and that a qualification of *actus aper* is missing, such as *Laurens ille canum siluestri e tegmine morsu*.' One may note that vv. 58, 59, 60, and *Aen.* 10.707—which corresponds to the missing verse—all end in -*is*: this must have encouraged haplography.

As Heinsius acutely saw, the Ms. *seruit*, if it represents *se ruit*, requires the subordination of the preceding clause.

60   IRAM DENUNTIAT: this seems to be reminiscence of *Aen.* 3.366, *Celaeno . . . tristis denuntiat iras*. In that passage—as in *Geo.* 1.453, [*sol*] *caeruleus pluuiam denuntiat*, and Prop. 4.3.61, *illa dies . . . caedem denuntiat agnis*—there seems to be a notion of futurity that is hardly to be understood in our passage. The use of the prosaic verb *denuntiare* must be considered remarkable and un-Ovidian. According to the *ThLL* (5.552.70) the only uses in the poets, other than those given above, are *Aetna* 236 and Lygd. 5.5. For the use of the ablative with *denuntiare*, cf. *oculis et adspectu denuntiare*, Cic. *leg. agr.* 2.13, etc.

SAETIS . . . HIRTIS: metrical reasons dictate the placing of the adjective at the end of the line, but it is likely that Ovid would have avoided putting the unemphatic adjective in this emphatic place.

61   SE RUIT: *et ruit* is a convenient reading here, and it disposes of the difficulty in connecting the sentences. Yet it is difficult to see how the simple *et ruit* could have been altered into *seruit*, particularly as the verb *seruire* would not seem to be suggested by the context. It further would seem to require that we take both *nitens* and *ruit* with *in uulnera*. Consequently I incline to the view of Heinsius and

Vollmer that the text should be read as *se ruit*.[1] *se ruit . . . in uulnera* seems to echo Lucan 6.222, *se rotat in uulnus*. Cf. commentary on v. 58. Whether a colon should be read at the end of v. 60, as Vollmer proposes, or whether the words I believe to have been lost before v. 60 contained the clue to the connexion, I cannot say, but Heinsius' suggestion of *dum nuntiat* seems very unlikely, as the parallels support *denuntiat*, and the simple *nuntiat* is very flat.

NITENS IN UULNERA: if the reading above is correct, the word *se* is the object of *ruit*, and the participle here is not otiose as Birt (p. 21) claims. The force of *nitens* may be compared with *conixa*, v. 28, as indicating the notion of 'thrusting' oneself rather than simply leaning. The phrase has a hint of oxymoron.

62   PRESSUS: the natural way to take this word would seem to be as 'harassed',[2] much the same as *oppressus* (*simplex pro composito*, cf. *sidit*, v. 24), cf. the active uses: *sic me ferus ille premebat*, M 5.604; *nos premat . . . bello tellus*, *EP* 1.7.11. The difficulty is that this does not seem to suit the context very well, as the emphasis is no longer on the fact that the boar is harassed. Still, the idea in *actus* may be repeated. O. Skutsch, however, suggests that *pressus* may be taken as 'pressed on the spear by the force of his onrush', and hence almost *se imprimens*; cf. [Xen.] *Cyn.* 10.16, quoted a few lines below.

ET: cf. Appendix I.

EMISSO: as it seems the event being discussed is the self-impaling of a boar on a hunting spear[3] (cf. [Xen.] *Cyn.* 10.16, ὁ δ' [ὗς] ὑπὸ τοῦ μένους πρόσεισι, καὶ εἰ μὴ κωλύοιεν οἱ κνώδοντες τῆς λόγχης, ἀφίκοιτ' ἂν διὰ τῆς ῥάβδου προσωθῶν αὐτόν . . .), any reference to verbs of throwing seems to be out of place (cf. Fränkel, p. 262). Yet, as *emitto* seems to lose any notion of separation from an agent in some passages, we may read it here. Cf. *Ep.* 14.107, *per septem Nilus portus emissus in aequor*, where *emissus* seems to mean 'having issued forth' (cf. Liv. 26.40.11) and would rather support Wernsdorf's theory that the spear stuck right through the boar, and out the other side. In Celsus 7.22.3, *acus per membranam emittitur* [*FV: immittitur J*], and Celsus 4.1.7, [*iunctura*] . . . *portae modo in inferiores partes ea . . . emittit*, there is evidence to make us think that *emitto* tended to mean

---

[1] Cf. Apul. *flor.* 2, p. 8, *quorsus potissimum in praedam superne sese ruat*, and Ter. *Eun.* 599, *foras simul omnes proruont se.*   Scanty support!

[2] *premo* was a technical term of the hunters, cf. Forcellini, s.v., and Enk on Gratt. 205: 'Premere est ita prope insequi feram, ut elabi non possit', ii.70.

[3] Gratt. 108 *et sq.* also describes the scene:

> *ille etiam ualido primus uenabula dente*
> *induit, et proni moderatus uolneris iram*
> *omne moris excepit onus.*

immitto, and that our text *emisso . . . per uiscera telo* means 'a weapon having been thrust in through his entrails'. *eniso* with much the same sense may be supported by a passage in Seneca: *nat.* 4.2.14 [*molliorem crocodilorum partem inferiorem*] *delphini spinis, quas dorso eminentes gerunt, submersi uulnerabant, et in aduersum enisi diuidebant.* This involves taking the spear as an active agent, and hence seems less likely.

63 ALTERA PARS: this marks the transition to a class of animal impelled by nature to fly from pursuers. It is remarkable that three examples (Ovid was fond of triple exemplification—Owen, *CQ* 8 (1914), p. 261) are given, just as in the previous lines, but, no doubt from the nature of the case, the treatment is very brief.

SEQUENTI: does this imply hunters? Unfortunately the context is not such that we can be certain, and the question is of some importance in considering Keydell's interpretation of v. 52. It would seem to be best to take it of any person or beast that preyed on the timid animals. For the use of the participle as a noun, cf. v. 22.

64 UT: cf. Appendix 1.

TERGORE: Birt (p. 33) shows that *tergus* (for *tergum*) is found only twice in the Metamorphoses and once in Vergil,[1] and only in *M* 13.347 is it used in the sense of *pellis.*[2] It seems that here (and possibly in vv. 95 and 126) the meaning is 'skin' or 'hide'.[3] It must be admitted that the three occurrences here are not in the manner of Ovid. Propertius, however, has *aurea quam molli tergore uexit ouis* (2.26.6), and the imitation in *Ep.* 17.144 reads *quem . . . aurea lanigero uellere uexit ouis.* Postgate *ad loc.* also compares Manilius 4.518, *Colchida tergore uexit.* It would seem that the word, although avoided by Virgil and Ovid, was not the subject of a general poetic convention.[4]

65 CAPTO . . . TIMORE: this is a rather difficult phrase. Gesner took it as a substitute for *concepto timore* (cf. Lucan 6.659, *trepida conceptos mente timores,* and *F* 1.485), used as (he claims) *capiunt . . . palmam* in v. 67. Such a use is common in Ovid: *spem capere, M* 12.506; *capitur nunc mente uoluptas, EP* 4.9.37, etc. The *ThLL* (3.329.24) understands this passage as *pati, subire,* and compares *Aen.* 6.352, *. . . iuro non ullum pro me tantum cepisse timorem, quam . . . ; M* 9.617, *nec taedia coepti ulla mei capiam*; and a few other passages.[5] These alternatives seem to me sufficiently to support the reading of *capto* here, and to

---

[1] *M* 8.649; 13.347; *Aen.* 1.211.
[2] The English equivalent 'hide' also is devoid of poetic quality.
[3] Cf. Pliny 9.95 where *tergus* is used of the crab's shell.
[4] Cf. Sil. 3.209; Gratt. 339.
[5] For passive cf. Ps.-Cic. *exil.* 22, *mors . . . quae ob rem publicam capitur*; Hirt. *gall.* 8.30.2.

render Heinsius' *cauto* unnecessary. In any case *cauto* implies a certain amount of reason or foresight, which is not the same as the idea in v. 50, *uani timores*, and v. 64, *pauidi*.

SINE FINE: this common Ovidian tag seems badly placed here. It results in two ablatives at the end of the line (and three final syllables in *e*). (Birt quotes: *deposito pariter cum ueste timore* (*Ep.* 17.57), which reads not too badly, and *non alte percusso corde sagitta* (*M* 6.266), where the change in genders is of assistance.) The separation of *sine fine* from the verb *fugiens*, which this phrase seems to modify, is awkward. The meaning of *sine fine* is 'without limit', as in *Ibis* 207, *illae me lacrimae facient sine fine beatum*; hence here *fugiens . . . sine fine* may be taken as 'fleeing amain'.

65a As indicated above, on v. 52, I believe that v. 52 (65a) properly should be read here. The early editors do not seem to have had any reason for preferring to read the verse at 52 rather than at this place. However, if the verse is to be read here, it must be preceded by a lacuna, for there is no connexion with what goes before. It would seem from the emphatic statement at v. 82, *noster in arte labor positus, spes omnis in illa*, that it must have been stated earlier in the poem that the work of the huntsman lay partly in *ars* (cf. *artis*, Gratt. 1), but that he was aided by the horse and the hound and that they did not entirely rely on skill but partly on natural instinct, i.e. *ipsa sequi natura monet uel comminus ire*. The following scheme of our poem then becomes clear, with the hackneyed contrast between *natura* and *ars*:

1– 8 All animals have *natural* knowledge of powers.
9–48 The natural cunning of fishes.
49–51 Introduction to land animals.
53–62 The natural foolhardiness of some land animals;
63–65 the natural timidity of other land animals.
(*lost*: the hunter trains the horse and the hound, but nevertheless)
65a their very *nature* instructs them to chase or fight.
66–74 This is the greater glory of the mettlesome horse, *and*
75–81 the chief praise of the hounds who are brave fighters, keen trackers, and stern chasers . . . and even urge on the master, following the quarry afar.
(*lost*: on the sea we have no dogs or horses to aid us)—
81 all our work, all our hope, is in '*art*'.

O. Skutsch objects to my interpretation on the following grounds: (*a*) If *generosus* is to be taken with *equorum*, it should then be an ornamental, and not a qualifying, adjective; (*b*) *quin laus prima canum* cannot naturally be taken to mean *laus prima canum est natura eorum* (v. 75); (*c*) my taking *quibus . . . sequendi* (vv. 75–6) as a parenthesis is a harsh consequence of (*b*) and counter to the natural development of v. 75 in vv. 75–6.

I admit these difficulties, but think it is possible that a reader who had the original text, before it was so obscured by *lacunae*, may have found the sequence of thought easier to follow. I do not find Skutsch's alternative interpretation more convincing than my own:

post 65   ⟨*quae uero seruire sibi et sufferre laborem*
          ars hominum docuit ratioque infusa coegit⟩
          ipsa sequi natura monet uel comminus ire.

(Domesticated animals are governed by their nature as modified by their training.)

75–81   *quae laus prima canum*, etc.: this nature modified by training is the chief praise of the hounds—with examples.

66–74   *hic generosus honos et gloria maior equorum*, etc.: this combination of nature and training is the nobility and the glory, which in their case is even greater (than in that of the hounds), of the horses—with examples.

(*lost*: but *natura* plays no part in fishing)

82   *noster in arte labor positus, spes omnis in illa.*

(Cf. *Ovidiana*, p. 450 *et sq.*) This interpretation involves making *gloria* in v. 66 include the meaning *amor gloriae*, for in Skutsch's view it is *amor gloriae* that the examples illustrate.

IPSA . . . NATURA: it is impossible to say whether the author had any notion of personification here.

66 HIC: i.e. *ipsa natura (eorum)*, but, of course, *hic* is attracted to the gender of *honos*. To the objection of O. Skutsch that no one would claim that the horse is inspired by its nature to pursue or give combat (*Ovidiana*, p. 452), and that consequently lines 66–74 should be placed *post* 81, I would reply that *sequi uel comminus ire* may have referred to something in the lacuna, and that the author picked up the idea of *natura* for its own sake, so that it could be contrasted with *ars* in v. 82.

GENEROSUS: it seems best to take this word as referring, by hypallage, to *equorum*. So *ThLL* 6.1801.46, cf. *generosi ac nobiles equi* (Sen. *clem.* 1.24.2) (Vergil uses the word with *pecus*, *Geo.* 3.75.)

HONOS: the recurrence of the -*or*[1] sound, rather than any scruples about prosody, is probably the cause for avoiding *honor* here. Ovid would have allowed the lengthening of the last syllable of *honor*; cf. Axelson, p. 26; M. Schmidt, *De Ovidii versibus hexametris* (Prog. Cleve, 1856), p. 25; Vollmer, *SBA*, 1917, 3te Abh., p. 12.

---

[1] For a similar avoidance of jingle, cf. *M* 13.96, *quam mihi, maior honos, coniunctaque gloria nostra est.* Ovid seems to have a slight preference for *honor, ceteris paribus*. Cf. *ThLL* 6.2916.36.

HONOS ... GLORIA: no doubt to be taken in the simple sense referring to the quality which is the cause of 'honour' and 'glory', cf. *laus*, v. 75.

MAIOR: their strength and their fleetness are great sources of honour to the *generosi equi*, but by comparison their *natura* is *maior* still, cf. notes on v. 75. The horse's *indoles* comes first in Verg. *Geo.* 3.75 and Colum. 6.29.1.

generosi equi were suited *by nature* for the Circus and its races and *uenationes*: cf. Colum. 6.27.1, *est enim generosa materies quae circo sacrisque certaminibus equos praebet.* Cf. *ibid.* (29.1), *cum uero natus est pullus confestim licet indolem aestimare: si hilaris, si intrepidus . . . haec erunt honesti animi documenta*; and then a long list of physical qualities is given.

67 NAM: I take this word as introducing the justification of the statement in v. 66 that the horses' spirit is a source of glory to them.

CUPIUNT: I have adopted this reading of Birt's because I feel it expresses more cogently the nature of the horse to seek glory which is illustrated in the lines following; *cupiunt* seems better to accord with *gaudent*. Palaeographically it is very probable.[1]

For *cupiunt animis* cf. Cat. 15.3, *si quicquam animo tuo cupisti*; Cat. 64.145, *aliquid cupiens animus praegestit apisci.* For *capiunt animis* (to contain, ?to comprehend) cf. *RA* 392, *capiunt animi carmina multa mei*; Lucan 1.184, [*Caesar*] *ingentes . . . animo motus bellumque futurum ceperat.*

TRIUMPHO: this word is probably vaguely used, and hardly refers to the actual horses which drew the triumphal car. The force here need be nothing more than *uictoria*, cf. Cic. *Vat.* 39, *tribules ita* [*te*] *oderunt ut repulsam tuam triumphum suum duxerint.*

68 SEU: it is not impossible that, as Vlitius maintains, a previous alternative may be missing and that a gap should be shown in the text. Still, the correlation of *seu* and *ue cum* (v. 71) will be defended in Appendix 1. Then we must take the two sentences *nonne uides . . . aurae* and *quam tumidus . . . opimis* as parenthetic illustrations of the two alternatives in v. 68 and v. 71. Gesner took vv. 69–74 as all being subordinate to *nonne uides.* He must have been influenced by the subjunctive in his reading, *conpescat* (v. 73), and he had to read *ueniat* in v. 72. My reading of *conspissat* in v. 73 renders such a construction very unlikely. Any suggestion to punctuate after *gaudent*, and correlate *triumpho* and *circo*, is intolerably harsh, and scarcely has any basis of reality: a horse could hardly merit a crown in the triumph!

[1] Cf. Prolegomena, p. 5.

MERUERE CORONAM: cf. Verg. *Aen.* 5.355, *primam . . . merui . . .
coronam*, and Gratt. 288, *excitat . . . primae spes ambitiosa coronae.*

69 NONNE UIDES: this is a common tag: Lucr. 2.196, Gratt. 62,
Verg. *Geo.* 1.56, *M* 15.382, 5.375.

UICTOR: predicative, cf. Hor. *epist.* 1.10.37, *postq̄uam uictor uiolens
[equus] discessit. . . .*

SUBLIMIUS: as this occurs next to *altum* we may, perhaps, presume
the meaning is 'spiritedly', cf. *F* 1.301, *Venus et uinum sublimia pectora
fregit.* The adverbial form *sublimiter* is rare—Forcellini quotes only
two examples[1] excluding late usages. For the comparative, cf.
sublatior—a compound of the same preposition, and in the same part
of the verse (v. 55). Cf. *Geo.* 3.108, *illi [equi] . . . iamque elati* sublime
uidentur aera per uacuum ferri. . . . For *sublimius* in this sense one
may compare the passage from Donatus quoted *supra* on v. 55.
(Cf. *sublime elatos*, Liv. 21.30.8.)

ALTUM . . . CAPUT: this was a mark of a thoroughbred, cf. Oppian,
Cyn. 1.178. Note also *celsa . . . terga*, v. 71. Cf. *Aen.* 5.375, *Dares
caput altum in proelia tollit.*

70 UULGI . . . AURAE: 'to the favour of the commonalty'—cf.
Aen. 6.816, *iam nimium gaudens popularibus auris.* The *ThLL* (2.1471.60)
remarks that the word *aura* is especially poetic.

SE UENDITET: the perfect translation of this phrase would seem to
be the current slang 'he sells himself' in the sense of 'he wins
popularity by emphasizing his attractive qualities'. The use is quite
common in prose (e.g. Cic. *Att.* 1.16.16, *ualde te uenditaui:* I have
'puffed' you; *quomodo . . . se uenditant Caesari?* Cic. *Att.* 8.16.1; there is
often an idea of 'showing off'—e.g. *uenditatio . . . atque ostentatio*, Cic.
Lael. 86; *ingenii uenditandi aut memoriae ostentandae causa*, Rhet. Her.
2.30.47—which may be present here). I have not been able to trace
uenditare used thus in the poets,[2] and it seems likely that the associa-
tions of the phrase rendered it unsuitable for poetry. *uendo* is used in
this sense in Hor. *epist.* 2.1.74,

> *si uersus paulo concinnior unus et alter
> iniuste totum ducit uenditque poema,*

(I should imagine *ducit* may have been some similar usage), in
Prop. 1.2.3,

> *[quid iuuat] Orontea crinis perfundere murra
> teque peregrinis uendere muneribus?*

---

[1] Cato, *agr.* 70; Colum. 8.11.1.

[2] With the possible exception of Claudian 26.567. (But in hexameters only 3rd
person singular would scan, so it would naturally be rare.) For the iterative form
see footnote to commentary on *increpitant*, v. 80, *inf.*

(hardly any allusion to the trade of the *meretrix*) and in Juvenal 7.135,

> *purpura uendit causidicum, uendunt amethystina*

(but not, as Lewis and Short allege, Tib. 1.4.59).

The colloquial tone of the passages and works from which these instances are drawn should be noted.

71 CAESO ... LEONE: I take *leone* here as *pelle leonis* by synecdoche. Cf. Val. Flacc. 8.126, *aptans humeris capitique leonem*; Stat. *Ach.* 1.417, *clipeos caesis uestire iuuencis*, and also, *[puppis] caeso ... inducta iuuenco*, Lucan. 4.132 (cf. Verg. *Aen.* 5.329). *decoratur* read by Sannazaro seems to be ruled out by the change of subject to *ungula*, and it is unnecessary, though perhaps more poetic.

TERGA: poetic plural—cf. *F* 2.695, *et saepissime*.

72 For TUMIDUS as 'conceited', cf. *M* 1.754, *es tumidus genitoris imagine falsi*.

QUAM ... QUANTO: the construction changes to an exclamation after the rhetorical question.[1] It is a curious coincidence that on a similar passage (Opp. *Cyn.* 1.206) Mair notes: 'The distinction between the rhetorical interrog. and the exclamation disappears in late Greek.'

UENIT: (for the mood here, cf. note on v. 68) 'comes' (not 'is'— cf. Van Wageningen, *Mn.* 2.47 (1919), p. 343), cf. *redeuntis*, v. 74, and *concita*, v. 73.

SPECTABILIS: perhaps with a notion of 'surprising, wonderful' (cf. Magnus, *Hermes* 39 (1904), p. 39).

ACTU: this word primarily has the idea of motion, yet in view of the emphasis on the horse's anxiety to impress, we may see a secondary force predominant here—that of the 'actions' of the orator, cf. *EP* 3.5.15,

> *felices quibus haec ipso cognoscere in actu*
> *et tam facundo contigit ore frui.*

Presumably tossing the head, stamping the ground, and so on, as here indicated, are what is meant.

73 CONSPISSATQUE: I believe that this is the correct reading and that the palaeographical history is somewhat as follows:

---

[1] Hardly dependent on *nonne uides*, v. 69: cf. on v. 68.

(1) confusion of *s* and *n*: *conpissatque*.
    (Cf. *sanguiṣne*, v. 123; *mestes*, v. 51; possibly *his* for *in*, v. 46; and *si* for *n*, v. 108.)
(2) parasitic *c* arising from merovingian *a* (cf. *tenerco* for *tenera*, v. 3) : *conpisscatque*.
(3) loss of *i*: *conpsscatque*.
(4) restoration of *i*: *conpiscatque*.

Conspissare is a rare word, but *solum . . . conspissatum* is found in Colum. 2.18.5 (cf. *creta . . . conspissata*, Pliny 35.36).

If, as I believe, the author had in his mind the phrase in Vergil, *cauatque tellurem* (*Geo.* 3.87), once he thought of *solum* (rather more natural than *tellus*, I think), some semi-technical everyday phrase involving *conspissat solum* may have come to his mind. When one considers such words as *crinalis* (cf. notes on v. 31) and *nocuus* (cf. notes on v. 130), it will be admitted that this unusual word may well have been used here. For long I thought that *conpescatque* was the correct reading here, but the syntax makes it almost impossible to read the subjunctive, and, for palaeographic reasons, a correction to the indicative seems improbable. As O. Skutsch (*Ovidiana*, p. 451) remarks, most of the proposed readings are palaeographically improbable, and semantic objections can be urged against *conpisat* and *concrispat* (and, of course, against Sannazaro's *conspissat*!). His own *constipat* is not impossible, but I do not find it convincing. His further emendation—namely, to read *ue* for *que*—is, to my mind, very improbable, for it involves taking *ue* with the main verb, although both the form of the parallel sentences (*seu septem* (68); *celsaue cum* (71)) and simple logic require that it should go with the participle *redeuntis*. I do not dispute that the passage would be immensely improved if it were possible to read *ue*, for we would have three neat examples instead of the two rather awkward ones in our text as the Ms. gives it.

GENEROSO CONCITA PULSU: one would normally expect these words to mean 'sped with a noble impulse' from the position of *concita*, not to mention the analogies of such passages as *M* 6.158, *diuino concita motu*, and *acri concitus ira*, v. 39. And that *pulsus* can have this abstract meaning (rather like 'emotion') is clear from Cic. *diu.* 2.126, *siue . . . externus . . . pulsus animos dormientium commouet, siue per se ipsi animi mouentur*. Still, a comparison with the Vergilian passages where this word is used makes one incline to the view that *pulsu pedum* is meant ('stamping, kicking, drumming of hooves'):

Geo. 4.49, *ubi concaua pulsu saxa sonant* [sc. *pedum*].
Aen. 6.591, [*Salmoneus fulmen*] *cornupedum pulsu simularet equorum.*
          7.722, *pulsuque pedum conterrita tellus.*

12.334, *gemit ultima pulsu Thraca pedum.*
12.445, *pulsuque pedum tremit excita tellus.*
12.533, *crebro super ungula pulsu incita . . .* [*Murranum*] *proculcat equorum.*

The singular unanimity of these passages, and the close verbal relationship with the last passage seem to make it clear that *pulsu pedum* is in question. The relationship seems to be closest with *Aen.* 12.533, and in that passage I believe *pulsu* is to be taken with *proculcat*, and is an instrumental ablative. This would incline me to believe that our text should also be understood to have *pulsu* as an instrumental ablative modifying *conspissat*. Yet our author could have taken the passage in Vergil as having *pulsu* as a sort of modal ablative modifying *incita*. If this is the case then we can read our text more naturally by taking *generoso concita pulsu* together—but to say that the hoof is 'sped with a noble kick' seems rather odd to me. This leaves *generoso* in a rather awkward sense, but we may compare the hypallage in v. 66 as well as Seneca *dial.* 10.18.4, [*nobilium equorum*] *generosam pernicitatem.*

74 UNGULA: singular for plural.[1]

SPOLIIS . . . OPIMIS: for the general use as 'rich spoils', cf. Verg. *Aen.* 10.449. The literal meaning seems to be impossible as the *spolia opima* were won on three occasions only—long before this period. I believe these words simply refer to the skin of the slain lion. Just as the armour stripped from the dead general was the real *spolia opima*, so the *spolia opima* here are the skin stripped from the vanquished king of the beasts.

GRAUITER: what does this word mean? One might guess from the *spoliis opimis* that the horse returned *grauiter onustus* with such trifles as the *caesus leo* (cf. *grauius onustum* (Apul. *met.* 4.4); and there is a passage in Vergil (*Geo.* 3.140) where Servius suggests as an alternative explanation that *aut* grauibus onustis *dicit*—of waggons drawn by pregnant mares). Yet there is such a close parallelism, in this line and the previous one, with the following passage, that it seems that our author has, once again remembering the sound rather than the sense, concocted his work from the *Georgics* (3.87),

> *cauatque*
> *tellurem et solido grauiter sonat ungula cornu,*

so it seems that we must take *grauiter redeuntis* as 'returning with a deep sounding gallop'! O. Skutsch (in *Ovidiana*, p. 451) compares

---

[1] Cf. Bednara, *ALL* 14 (1906), p. 564—first used by Ennius, imitated by many successors.

Quint. *inst.* 11.3.112, [*in scena*] *iuuenum, senum . . . grauior ingressus est . . . serui, ancillae . . . citatius mouentur,* and takes *grauiter* here as 'in a stately, dignified manner'.

REDEUNTIS: sc. *equi.* As *infra,* v. 81, the dactylic rhythm seems intentionally used for onomatopoeic effect. Possibly imitated from Vergil (*Geo.* 3.87, etc.).

75 QUI (Ms.): it seems certain that this word must be corrupt, for the only meaning one can give it is 'how?' or 'thus'; (cf. Neue-Wagener ii.458; this sense is not in Ovid: Leyhausen, p. 20). Neither of these senses seems to be possible here, and we should expect a positive statement parallel with that in v. 66. The reading of Logus (*quae*) is reasonable, for it balances the *hic* of v. 66, yet it seems peculiar that we should have a history like *quae—que—qui,* though not at all impossible. I think that Heinsius was nearer with his *quid?* or *dein,* for we seem to need something a little emphatic here. Hence I believe that Birt's (p. 43) *quin* is indicated by the context and suited to the palaeographic conditions.

For *quin* in this usage one may refer to Stolz-Schmalz, p. 784, where we read . . . 'in der Umgangsprache ganz die Bedeutung von *immo* angenommen hatte, vgl.' Donatus on Ter. *Eun.* 902, '*quin* pro *immo*', and p. 785, 'blosses *quin*' (for *quin etiam*) 'ist hauptsächlich dichterisch, z.B. Prop. 2.10.15'.

For the sentence here with the omission of *est* it would appear to be fair to compare the following passage: *Aen.* 7.321 (as a *final* point), *quin idem Veneri partus suus et Paris alter, funestaeque iterum recidiua in Pergama taedae.* Then my interpretation of these words will amount to: *quin* [*natura eorum*] *est prima laus canum,* and the following passage mentions their other merits, but stresses their keen spirit in tracking the game (77–8), in urging on their master (79), and chasing the quarry should it escape the hunter (80).

LAUS PRIMA CANUM rather suggests an echo of Grattius 151,

> *prima illa canum, non ulla per artis*
> *cura prior . . .*

AUDACIA PRAECEPS is considered a good quality as distinct from the *non sana ferocia mentis* (v. 51), *quae trahit in praeceps.* Cf. Gratt. 167, *praeceps uirtus.*

76 UENANDIQUE SAGAX UIRTUS: cf. Cic. *diu.* 1.65, *sagire sentire acute est, ex quo sagae anus, . . . et sagaces dicti canes,* and *nat. deor.* 2.158.

Vahlen's conjecture at Ennius *Ann.* 533 Vah., *inuictus canis nare sagax et uiribus fretus,* rather resembles our passage.

UIRES SEQUENDI: cf. *uires nocendi,* v. 43, *sup.*

77 QUAE NUNC ELATIS RIMANTUR NARIBUS AURAM: here we have

come to a description of an actual hunt, and the previous words are,
no doubt, parenthetic, so that what follows explains the statement
quin laus prima canum. quae is feminine plural, cf. Neue-Wagener
i.920, Feminine[1] used 'besonders von Jagdhunden, κυών ebenfalls
in dieser Anwendung gern Fem.'

ELATIS ... NARIBUS is a phrase in Ennius, *Ann.* 602, and Vergil,
Aen. 12.115.

RIMANTUR: cf. Tac. *Hist.* 4.11.1, *rimandis offensis sagax.*

naribus auras is a tag found in Lucr. 4.993 and Gratt. 239, *celsisue
adprensant naribus auras.* These tags make one suspect that we should
read *auras* with Sannazaro, but the Ms. *aurara* suggests that Haupt is
correct with *auram* (*aurā, aura, aurara,* cf. Havet §§ 739, 740). I
have been influenced by *aurae,* v. 70 (contrast *popularibus auris,
Aen.* 6.816), to decide finally in favour of Haupt.

78 ET NUNC: cf. Appendix 1.

DEMISSO QUAERUNT UESTIGIA ROSTRO: cf. *M* 1.536, [*canis*] *extento
stringit uestigia rostro.*

QUAERUNT: cf. [*canes*] *oculis* ... *Actaeona quaerunt, M* 3.243.

79 ET PRODUNT CLAMORE FERAM: cf. [Xen.] *Cyn.* 6.16–17,
'Ἐπειδὰν δὲ περὶ τὸν λαγῶ ὦσι, δῆλον ποιήσουσι τῷ κυνηγέτῃ σὺν ταῖς
οὐραῖς τὰ σώματα ὅλα συνεπικραδαίνουσαι . . . . . . ὁ δὲ ἐξαίφνης ἀνάξας
ὑλαγμὸν ποιήσει τῶν κυνῶν καὶ κλαγγὴν φεύγων.

PRODUNT: they 'discover', in the etymological sense; cf. *M*
13.106, *nitor galeae* ... *insidias prodet*; etc.

CLAMORE: Vergil uses *clamor* of *apes boues mergi uolucres.* Cf. Enk
on Grattius 239 (ii.79), who remarks that in Grattius the hound
bays when the lair of the beast is found, 'in Halieuticis uero de cane
inuestigante sermo est'. But I take it that the hound in the *Hal.*,
which has been tracking, has just found the quarry and bays back
the news to the hunter. How does Enk take *produnt*? Hardly *clan-
gore* (κλαγγῇ) for *clamore* (cf. Enk on Gratt. 186, ii.66).

80 INCREPITANT: this seems to be the key word in the illustration:
'they upbraid, they urge on' their slothful master. Thus the spirit of
the hounds is emphasized, because they are keener for the hunt than
the hunter himself. It is noteworthy that it is not explicitly stated
that the *dominus* tarries. I believe that our author has in mind two
passages from Seneca (cf. Appendix 5 and *Atti,* p. 37) which supplied the background to the picture he sketches here in outline
only.

---

[1] Enk on Gratt. 185, 'Cynegetici scriptores canes feminas nominare malunt
quam mares, quod illae multum sint animosiores' (ii, p. 66); but he says on Gratt.
155, 'Bene adnotat Vlitius ... "canes feminas hic omnes sagaces constituit, mares
bellicosos"' (ii, p. 58).

This notion of 'urging on' is strong in the verb *increpitare*[1] (cf. the gardener in the *Georgics* (4.138), *aestatem increpitans seram*), and is, no doubt, connected with the idea of 'reproach' in the word (cf. *Aen.* 1.738, and Servius *ad loc.*; also Val. Flacc. 5.267). So too in *M* 14.821 Ovid uses the simple verb for 'urge on': *conscendit equos Gradiuus et ictu uerberis increpuit* (he did not necessarily crack his whip—cf. Tib. 1.1.30); cf. also *A* 3.15.17.

QUAM: I read this word for the Ms. *quem* because (*a*) my interpretation of *collatis . . . armis* requires that those words be governed by *effugit*; hence *quem* as a direct object also governed by this verb would be awkward; (*b*) it is difficult to understand the subject of *effugit*, particularly with *insequitur* following; and (*c*) *insequitur* has no object.

My reading supplies an object for *insequitur*, implies the subject of *effugit*, and relieves the latter verb of the awkward double construction. (Vlitius' *quae* gives substantially the same sense.) The palaeographic change is very slight—cf. Prolegomena, p. 5, and variants at *Ibis* 36. For the parenthesis in which *dominumque uocando increpitant* stands, cf. *Aen.* 6.852, where either half of the line must stand in parenthesis.

CONLATIS . . . ARMIS: in the sixth chapter of the pseudo-Xenophontic *Cynegeticus* the method of hunting that seems to be intended here is fully detailed. *armis* evidently refers to the nets, which were set up in a semicircle, and into which the hunter tried to drive his quarry. The meaning 'nets' is often present in *arma*—but perhaps not exclusively—in passages about hunting: cf. Grattius 51, 78, 81, 93, etc. *conlatis* may be translated as 'placed around': cf. Nepos 7.10.4, *Bell. Alex.* 39.2, etc. Then we may translate *si conlatis effugit armis* as 'if it escapes from the nets placed around' and not as an ablative 'absolute': 'if it escapes when the nets have been set around', for the nets were set up before the hunting began at all (cf. also *Ovidiana*, p. 453). The method of hunting is also discussed by Enk on Grattius 24–33 (ii.18). For the general sense of *arma*, cf. *ThLL* 2.590.58.

Birt's (p. 26) assertion, that *conlatis armis* implies that the animal fought the hunter, and that thus *effugit* is incongruous, is wrong: cf. *arma confero*, in Caesar (*gall.* 7.11.2, *ciu.* 2.18.2, etc.), without any notion of a battle.

81 TUMULOSQUE . . . CAMPOSQUE PER OMNIS: cf. *Aen.* 2.498,

---

[1] 'Epic' poets, from Lucretius onward, substitute iterative for simple verbs, *metri gratia*, according to Wölfflin, *ALL* 4 (1877), pp. 197–222.

camposque per omnis; *tumulos* is, no doubt, just *collis*.[1] The dactylic rhythm seems to be used deliberately to represent the rapidity of the chase.

CANIS: the singular is required by the metre. Cf. plural [Xen.] *Cyn.* 6.19, and *increpitant*, v. 80.

OMNIS: this expansion (rather than *omnes*) of $\overline{oms}$ is supported by the haplography suggested in the next paragraph. Cf. *N.L.*, p. 160.

81a   OMNIS: this supplement by O. Skutsch (cf. *Ovidiana*, p. 453) seems to prove that there was a lacuna here. Certainly the transition is very abrupt, and the suggested repetition of *omnis* is quite in the manner of the author (cf. v. 7, *sup.*). For the haplography, cf. v. 91, *inf.*

82   NOSTER IN ARTE LABOR: if the interpretation that I have given of the previous lines (cf. notes on vv. 52 and 65a) is correct, then these words must mean 'our work lies in a craft' as distinguished from natural instinct. (For the age-old dichotomy of *ars* and *natura*, cf. Cic. *fin.* 4.10, *ars tamen certior est dux quam natura*; Sen. *contr.* 1, *pr.* 17, etc.). For the fisherman's *ars*, cf. *M* 3.588. *noster*: of the author and the reader; perhaps just *meus*.

For the omission of the copula 'in sententiis grauiter dictis', cf. Winter, p. 24 (but cf. p. 33): 'Nec minus saepe quam Vergilius, Ouidius in uersibus qui commotione quadam distinguuntur, ellipsi utitur', but admits that the Mss. are often uncertain in the tradition. Hilberg treats this question at length, pp. 388 *et sq.*, but Winter often differs from him.

POSITUS: cf. *te scilicet omnis in uno nostra salus posita est* (*M* 3.648).

SPES OMNIS IN ILLA: cf. Gratt. 2, *prius omnis in armis spes fuit*; Verg. *Aen.* 2.162, *omnis spes Danaum . . . Palladis auxiliis semper stetit*; cf. *Aen.* 11.308. Gesner has the remarkable notion that *illa* (*cane*) is meant here! Of course the natural interpretation is *illa* (*arte*).

Vollmer (p. 530) here puts the emphasis on *omnis* and says the contrast is with hunting where the hunter has the aid of dogs and horses; Vlitius also thinks the contrast is with hunting, and sees the contrast between the methods required to combat the brute force of land animals and the wiles of fishes. These views are really complementary. For *illa* at the end of the line, cf. *M* 15.454–5.

83   NEC TAMEN: these words make it quite clear that there must be a lacuna before these lines which contained something that implied the fisherman should venture out on the high seas.

Perhaps the missing passage gave as the first precept of the art the advice in Oppian 3.66 *et sq.*, that the fisherman should put to sea with a following

---

[1] But suggested by *cumulo* in *Aen.* 2.498; cf. *Atti*, p. 36.

breeze, and then the correction *nec tamen* was introduced; perhaps the advice was like that in Hor. *carm.* 2.10.1 *et sq.* where Licinius is advised not to hug the shore too closely.[1]

We have now come to a practical work, which dealt with fishing as a sport, or means of livelihood, and it is on a different plane from the philosophic speculation that we have read previously. The language of the following lines gives the practical reasons for finding out the nature of the sea-bed.

MEDIAS used of the high sea (but not always, cf. Serv. auct. *Aen.* 3.270, *medio apparet fluctu:* iuxta morem cottidianum dicit *medio*, ut si dicamus 'in medio mari naufragium fecit' cum interdum non longe a litore contingit).

TE: cf. *nonne uides*, v. 69; *noster*, v. 82. The ancients usually named the particular reader for whom a didactic work was supposed to be written. Perhaps someone was named in a lost dedication; we cannot be sure.

PERGERE: cf. v. 53, *sup.*, and *pergit in hostem, Aen.* 11.521; *pergentem ad litora*, Sil. 7.171; Liv. 3.6.7, etc.

SEDES: cf. *aetherias sedes, M* 15.839; *sidereas . . . sedes, AA* 2.39 (for the plural form, cf. Bednara, *ALL* 14 (1906), p. 554). *pelagi sedes* is a rather peculiar circumlocution for *pelagus*.

84 UASTI may best be taken in the sense of 'vast' in view of *profundum* following; cf. *ultima me uasti sustinet ora freti, EP* 3.4.58.

PROFUNDUM: normally used by itself to mean 'the deep sea'.[2] E. Schmidt compares Val. Max. 2.10.6 on p. 79, 'Ouidius (?) solum neutrum sing. cum gen. coniungit: *Hal.* 84 . . . Item Val. Max. . . . 'C. . . . Marius in profundum ultimarum miseriarum abiectus'. (*profundo maris*, Suet. *Tib.* 40, is a *falsa lectio*.)

85 INTER UTRUMQUE LOCI MELIUS MODERABERE FINEM: I can only suggest that this line should be read as an example of hyperbaton meaning *inter utrumque loci finem melius moderabere (nauem)*, i.e. between the shallow waters and the deep sea. One may compare v. 65, *et capto fugiens ceruus sine fine timore*, for the hyperbaton. *moderari* seems to have a notion of *nauem gubernare*: cf. Stat. *Theb.* 10.14,

> *ceu mare per tumidum uiduae moderantibus alni*
> *quas deus et casus tempestatesque gubernant.*

All the other conjectures seem to make it necessary to read *inter utrumque loci* as a single phrase. I have no authority whatever for

[1] I do not agree with Bücheler, *RhM* 51 (1896), p. 326, that Ps. Sol. *Pont.* 21, *fac saltem primas pelagi libemus harenas*, shows that the author read the *Hal.*
[2] On the use as a noun *only* (and *not* as an adjective), cf. Housman ad Lucan, 1.455.

6—H.

this, and it seems a most improbable phrase indeed: 'between either
of the place' (*inter utrumque locum*, or even *locorum*, would, of course,
be without objection).

H. Bauer has attempted (*Glotta* 10 (1920), p. 123) to defend *inter
utrumque loci*, and it cannot be denied that Ovid has some peculiar
uses of the genitive, but I do not feel that I could be convinced by
his reasoning:

> 'Ovid wagt Hal. 85 nach *intereā loci* ein *inter utrumque loci* zu bilden, weil
> er in dieser alten Wendung ein *eǎ* hörte. (Eine zweite Neuerung ist die
> räumliche Auffassung von *loci*, die bei Plautus und Terenz in diesen
> Wendungen nicht vorkommt. In dem Verse ist *finem* im Schluss mit Merkel
> in *linum* zu ändern. Wie Birt, de. hal., p. 26, *loci... moderabere finem*
> verstanden hat, ist mir nicht klar geworden.) Mit hinzutretendem Genitiv
> kennen schon Plautus und Terenz die Verbindung Präposition + Neutrales
> Pronomen: *post id locorum*; *in id loci=in eum locum*; daneben *ibi(dem) loci*
> (das spätere *eo loci* ist eine Vermengung von *ibi loci* und *eo loco*.)'

Birt took *inter utrumque* together. This is a common Ovidian phrase,
but we have little to explain what was meant here, as the context is
lost. Yet, as Bauer says, *loci melius moderabere finem* ('you will better
regulate the extremity of the place') is a very difficult phrase to
understand: why *finem*? why the singular? how can one be said to
regulate it?

But if one can read *inter utrumque loci* together (the cacophony of
inter utrumque locum seems to rule it out), then Merkel's *melius
moderabere linum* seems to give good sense, and is well supported by
M 13.923, *moderabar harundine linum*. What exactly is meant by
funem, which Bersmannus suggests, I cannot say: perhaps a cable
to pull the net (*AA* 1.764), perhaps part of the helmsman's gear
(Veg. *mil.* 4.46).

86 This verse clearly depends on some word that stated or
implied a question in the missing verse that preceded.

NAM explains the instruction in the lacuna (*uidendum est*, or the
like).

LENTOS: especially used of osiers and such that are both tough and
pliable; cf. *lentos... retendit arcus, M* 2.419.

87 DEPOSCUNT: this verb involves the personification (uncon-
scious, of course) of *talia loca*; the use of the English 'demand' is
very similar. Cf. Sen. *epist.* 76.20, *amor enim, ira, cupiditas pericula
depoposcerunt*, also Silius 3.226. The verb is found only once in
Ovid, *M* 1.200, *studiisque ardentibus ausum talia deposcunt*, and the
occurrence of *talia* in either passage suggests a reminiscence by our
author here.

CALAMOS: no doubt for the unmetrical Latin *harundines* (very common in the poets: *RA* 208, etc.); note that Pliny (32.12) when paraphrasing v. 36 does not use the Greek *calamo*, but the Latin *harundine*.

LITUS, which we might otherwise imagine to be the 'beach', here clearly has the meaning of the 'coastal sea-bed' (cf. notes on v. 125 and v. 134, *inf.*). Now Erik Wistrand[1] shows how *litus* can apply to the 'beach' as understood in English, to landing places, to strands covered by the sea for a time, and to coastal water. In our passage (which Wistrand does not discuss) none of these meanings seems to suit. A ship could hardly sail over such portion of the Mediterranean coast as would be covered by the very slight tides,[2] and here the meaning 'coastal shallow waters' will hardly suit, for what seems to be meant by *purum litus* is a bed free from rocks and weeds, not clear waters. There are a few passages in Wistrand which *may* be taken in this sense.

Ti. Donatus on *Aen.* 6.162: *in litore sicco: id est in harena litoris sicci (est enim et udum litus, ubi pelagus terminatur)*: this latter may mean the strip of sand just by the sea's edge; cf. the ambiguity between the 'sea-bed' and 'coastal waters' in Sen. *contr.* 2.1.13. But, as Wistrand remarks generally (p. 39), poetic texts like ours present added difficulty due to metonymy, etc.

88 MONS . . . CELSIOR: the singular form, and the comparative degree, are both unexpected, for they are not parallel to *aspera loca* and *uada*, and may be attributed to the influence of the metre. Ovid, according to the *ThLL* (3.772.31) is the first author who uses *celsior* (*M* 1.178).

HORRENTES DEMITTAT . . . UMBRAS: 'to cast down quivering shadows', is a very effective phrase, and the suggestion of Riese that *torrentes undas* should be read can hardly be accepted for two reasons; first, as Birt points out (p. 105), although Oppian does not set out in his catalogue the fish which abide in the shadowy places of the sea, nevertheless he incidentally mentions a number of fish which love the shade (cf. 4.422, 4.438 and 1.605); and, secondly, the phrase *horrentes umbras*, with its imitation of *Aen.* 1.165 (cf. 1.311), corresponds to the other Vergilian phrases in the poem. Cf. Appendix 5.

DEMITTAT: Birt (p. 106) compares Vitruv. 3.5.5, *lineae demittendae*, but cf. also the use for such phenomena as falling rain—*M* 2.310, [*pater omnipotens*] . . . *tunc habuit nec, quos caelo demitteret, imbres* . . .

---

[1] *Nach innen oder nach aussen?* . . . von Erik Wistrand (Göteborg, 1946), — see Anhang I. *Litus* (pp. 36–42).

[2] Even at Venice only a few feet; elsewhere measured in inches.

(although the Mss. vary here, and at *M* 1.261, *demittere* is clearly correct, cf. *Geo.* 1.23). This verb would fit Riese's conjecture just as well, cf. *quo se demittere riui adsuerant*, *M* 8.334.

89 NAM: how do the words that follow explain the necessity of looking out for the shadowy places in the sea?—'for some avoid and seek variously', i.e. 'some fish seek the shade, others avoid it, thus they act in different ways' (*uarie*).

UARIE is a rare word in the poets (once in Ovid: *F* 4.309), and can hardly be taken in any sense other than as in v. 92, *inf.*, 'in different ways': cf. Sall. *Cat.* 61.9, *ita uarie per omnem exercitum laetitia maeror luctus atque gaudia agitabantur*.

QUIDAM: 'certain fishes'; hardly, as Birt (pp. 26, 28) suggests, *quaedam* (different things) for that is a general truth which gives the cause of writing the whole passage at all, and, as he realized (p. 105), involves transposing vv. 88–9 *ante* 86.

FUGIUNTQUE PETUNTQUE: an Ovidian tag, *AA* 1.545; cf. also *T* 1.2.31. On *que . . . que*, cf. Christensen *ALL* 15 (1908), p. 165 *et sq.*, and especially p. 205 where the use with contrasting verbs is illustrated—e.g. *sequiturque fugitque* (*M* 4.461); *parentque iubentque* (*M* 8.636).

90 UADA for *mare* occurs first in Catullus according to Bednara (*ALL* 14 (1906), p. 551) and the singular only is found in Plautus and Terence. Here it must mean the 'sea bed'; cf. Pliny 9.85 [*polypi*] . . . *uada non adprehendunt* translating Ar. 524 a 20 [πουλύπους] ἐὰν δ' εἰς τὴν ἄμμον ἐμπέσῃ οὐκέτι δύναται κατέχειν. O. Skutsch suggests, however, that, in the *Halieutica*, *uada* may nevertheless mean 'shallow water', and that *ab* should be supplied with *imo*: 'the water is made green by plants that have grown up from the bottom'. The line might have been conceived as *num uada subnatis herbis uiridentur ab imo* and then negligently recast to the present form.

SUBNATIS: cf. Pliny 17.148, [*castaneae nuces*] . . . *solutae sponte cadunt ex arbore, atque subnascuntur*. For *nascor* used of plants, cf. Ovid, *M* 1.108, *mulcebant Zephyri natos sine semine flores*.

IMO: Birt claims (p. 27) that it is necessary to have a noun with this adjective, and concludes that in a lacuna after the line some such word as *gurgite* occurred. This does not seem necessarily to follow. Cf. *ex imo*, *M* 11.499. One would prefer *in* (or *ab*) *imo* here. Cf. Appendix 2, *ad fin.*

UIRIDENTUR: the active form *uiridare* in all other passages is found in an intransitive sense, with the exception of Val. Flacc. 6.134–6,

> *non ego sanguineis gestantem tympana bellis*
> *Thyrsageten cinctumque uagis post terga silebo*
> *pellibus, et nexas uiridantem floribus hastas,*

where we can hardly presume that he was 'green in respect of his spears', as this would involve a double transference: 'the green flowers made the spear green, and the spear made Thyrsagetes green' —normally the use of the Greek accusative is restricted to 'Körperteilnamen' and in such cases the use is quite clearly an accusative of extent (Stolz-Schmalz, p. 379). E. Merone, *Sulla lingua di Valerio Flacco* (Naples, 1957), pp. 25, 27, does not consider this possibility, and takes *uiridantem* as transitive. Our passage is the only example of the passive. André, p. 242, remarks that verbs (derived from names of colours) . . . 'en *are* sont tantôt transitifs (*rufare*), tantôt intransitifs (*internigrare*). Ils sont même souvent les deux à la fois, ainsi *in(d)albare, nigrare, rutilare, uiridare*'. Hence we may take *uiridare* as transitive here. *dealbare* (Cicero) and *infuscare* (Verg. *Geo.* 3.389, etc.) are among the transitive forms quoted by André (pp. 244–5). The verb is found in Vergil but does not occur at all in Ovid.

AB: cf. Appendix 2.

For HERBIS, 'sea-weed', cf. Sen. *nat.* 6.8.4, *implicatae aquis herbae*; Plin. *nat.* 2.227; 18.190; Auson. *Mos.* 74.

91 That there is a lacuna before v. 91 is fairly clear. It seems reasonable to assume that the missing line was one which started with *nam*, and was parallel to the other clauses above. As *nam* and *num* would be almost identical in appearance to the scribe (cf. Prolegomena, p. 5) his eye could easily be confused, and he would thus omit v. 90a. Birt's argument that the word *imo* in v. 90 requires *gurgite* in 90a has been considered, and he further argues that the subjunctives in this verse rule out *nam*. I do not think that either assertion necessarily follows—we could have something like *nam fit ut.* . . . Heinsius' (*imum*) *obiectetque moras et molli seruiat algae* has the advantage of giving the natural meaning to *obiectetque moras*, and takes *seruire* as *prodesse*. Birt (p. 28) believes that *piscis* is the subject; that *oblectat moras* means 'he whiles away the time'; and (it seems) that *molli seruiat algae* means 'he accommodates himself to the weed'. This is all very improbable.

92 DISCRIPSIT (evidently the correct word, cf. Housman ad Manil. 2.828), is rare in the poets, but Horace has two examples (*carm.* 2.13.23 (*v. l.*), *ars.* 86).

SEDES . . . PROFUNDI: cf. *pelagi . . . sedes*, v. 83. On *profundum* as a noun, cf. v. 84, *sup.*

NATURA: cf. v. 65a, *sup.* There is little doubt but that here we have *natura (rerum)*, although *natura profundi* is not impossible. For the idea here and in the next lines, cf. Oppian 1.93–5,

> 'ἰχθύσι μὲν γενεή τε καὶ ἤθεα καὶ πόρος ἅλμης
> κέκριται, οὐδέ τι πᾶσι νομαὶ νεπόδεσσιν ὁμοῖαι,
> οἱ μὲν γάρ. . .

93 CUNCTOS UNĀ: cf. v. 30; thus perhaps it is *una (sede)*, but the adverb seems more natural.

94 NAM GAUDENT PELAGO: these words bring us to the first portion of the catalogue which was introduced by vv. 92–3, and the poet proceeds to set out the names of fish that swim in the high seas. Note *pelagus*[1] here as the 'high sea', and contrast *medias pelagi . . . sedes*, v. 83.

QUALES: this may be corrupt, and perhaps we should read a fish-name: but cf. Appendix 1 (e).

BOUES: the Horned Ray—*Cephaloptera giorna* (*DT* 34); according to D'Arcy-Thompson it dwells in the mud, as Oppian states in 1.103. If this is correct, I do not see how D'Arcy-Thompson contents himself with the mild statement that in Ovid 'the allusion seems inappropriate, or obscure'.

95 MILUI: I hope to discuss the scansion elsewhere, but cf. Appendix 6. Lachmann[2] suggested that the reading here should be *iuli* (for the consequent elision, cf. *nomine asellus*, v. 133), but, as will be explained in Appendix 3 and in my commentary on v. 105, the argument of order in Pliny, and other considerations, make it certain that, linguistically desirable as would be the elimination of *milui* here, the recalcitrant facts prevent us from reading *iuli*. For the colour of the *miluus*, cf. Cotte: 'la couleur dorsale . . . est brune, avec des taches plus foncées, ce qui ne nous éloigne pas du texte d'Ovide' (p. 144). Cuvier, quoted by D'Arcy Thompson, describes it as *subfuscum* (*DT* 286). Are we to take *tergore* in the sense of 'back'? Cf. v. 126.

96 ET PRETIOSUS HELOPS: the action of most editors in printing *elops* here (under the influence of the Greek ἔλ[λ]οψ and the inferior Ms. B) is indefensible. The Ms. here, the best Ms. (B) in Pliny at the parallel passage, the predominant weight of Mss. evidence as shown in the *ThLL* (6.2597.76), and the specific testimony of Eutyches

---

[1] Cf. Greek οἱ πελάγιοι (ἰχθύες).
[2] On Lucr. 6.552 ('e Plinio').

(*apud* Cassiodorum Gramm. 7.201.9) (for what it is worth) all give *helops*.

NOSTRIS INCOGNITUS UNDIS, whence Pliny presumes it cannot be the *acipenser*; cf. v. 134, *inf*.

97 AC DURUS XIPHIAS: the Swordfish—*Xiphias gladius*; one would imagine that *durus* meant *crudelis* or *inmitis* in view of *ictu non mitior ensis*, yet it has generally been taken to refer to the texture of the flesh: cf. Xenocrates 9, βούγλωσσοι, ψῆττοι (sic Ideler), σκληρόσαρκοί (εἰσιν) and the Hippocratic *de uictus ratione* 2.48, οἱ δὲ πλανῆται καὶ κυματοπλῆγες τεθρυμμένοι τῷ πόνῳ στερεωτέρην καὶ βαθυτέρην τὴν σάρκα ἔχουσι . . . ; cf. also the discussion on *duri sues*, v. 132.

MITIOR: the use of this word for *ictus ensis*, even by implication, is strange, but *Ibis* 461, *domino non mitior illo*, probably occurred to the author as a convenient form. The etymological significance of this remark is clear; cf. Oppian 1.182, ξιφίαι τε φερώνυμοι.

98 AGMINE: Pliny uses this word to describe the shoals of Tunny in 9.50.

FUGIENTES: in view of the accounts in Pliny (9.50) we may take this word as referring to panic-stricken flight,[1] but it seems likely that we have the remains of an etymology of the word *thynnus* (cf. Oppian 1.181, θύννοι μὲν θύνοντες) which was in the source of our author.

99 PARUA ECHENAIS: for the Doric[2] form (contrast *echeneis* Pliny 9.79, etc.), cf. Pliny 32.148; Lucan 6.675 (and Housman *ad loc.*, who compares *polypus*), Don. Ter. *Eun.* 302 (*Andr.* 739). For its size, cf. Pliny 9.79, *est paruus admodum piscis, adsuetus petris, echeneis appellatus*, and Birt (p. 160). For the implied etymology, cf. Opp. 1.243, τοίων δὲ φερωνυμίην λάχεν ἔργων.

AT: confusion of *at* and *ad* was very common,[3] and the Ms. *adest* makes no sense,[4] so we must read *at est*.

MIRUM: the insertion of this word in clauses is common: e.g. *M* 7.790, *medio, mirum, duo marmora campo adspicio*.

MORA PUPPIBUS INGENS: since *nauibus* would read as easily, we may assume a deliberate desire for poetic colour, or that the poet was steeped in the poetic diction. This is the first account of the legendary

---

[1] *fugere* has not necessarily this implication—cf. Hor. *sat.* 2.7.35.

[2] Fohalle (R. Fohalle, 'Sur le vocabulaire maritime des Romains'—*Mélanges . . . Paul Thomas* (Bruges, 1930)) remarks that Ionic forms tended to predominate in the 'vocabulaire maritime' of the Greeks (p. 271).

[3] Quint. *inst.* 1.7.5; cf. Stolz-Schmalz, pp. 176–7.

[4] We cannot supply '*adest nobis canentibus*' (cf. *T.* 3.4.55, *sic tamen haec adsunt, ut quae contingere non est corpore: sunt animo cuncta uidenda meo*). This would break the sentence begun at v. 94.

power of the Remora[1] to hold back ships, but in view of the Greek and Latin names, and the superstitions that attached to the fish, there can be no doubt but the idea was widespread long before this poem was written.

INGENS: like the English 'great', often without a definite idea of size; cf. *Aen.* 12.926, *incidit ictus ingens.* There was a strong epic colour in this word, cf. Ingvarsson, *Eranos* 48 (1950), p. 66 *et sq.* (Cic. *Lael.* 98 is also interesting).

100 TUQUE: for the apostrophe, cf. v. 134, *tuque . . . acipenser,* and frequently in Ausonius' catalogue of fish in the *Mosella,* v. 91 *et al.* For Birt's proposal to transfer this line and the following one, *post* v. 117, cf. discussion on v. 101.

COMES RATIUM: cf. *T* 1.9.11, *utque comes radios per solis euntibus umbra est.* . . . Neue-Wagener, i.394, give the following occurrences of the genitive plural of *ratis*: Lucan 3.579, 3.706, 9.345; Ulpian *dig.* 4.9.1§4; Auson. *Mos.* 217. It seems from the following figures that Ovid (Birt, p. 37) and Vergil avoided the form:

	disyllabic cases	dative and abl. plural	gen. plural
apis Verg.	10	12	—
Ovid	13	—	1
auis Verg.	11	4	5
Ovid	83	6	5
ratis Verg.	20	5	—
Ovid	86[2]	4	—

Furthermore, when one considers how the Latin poets could express 'of the ships' in hexameter verse the avoidance becomes more obvious: *nauium, puppium, lintrium* were practically out of the question, and *carinarum* was very awkward, so that *ratium* was a word that seemed to be just inevitable. And yet, although the singular genitive which was not inevitable is found (*M* 11.493), the plural is not! I can but elaborate Birt's original observation and admit that the occurrence in the *Halieutica* seems to be a sign that Ovid was not the author; I cannot hazard any explanation of the apparent avoidance. De Saint-Denis (*LEC* 14 (1946), p. 55 *et sq.*) explains that *ratis* meant a kind of ship, and that the number of cases where it is freely used in a general sense is less than is usually supposed.

[1] On the etymology of this word, cf. Kretschmer, *Glotta* 1 (1909), p. 294; Richardson, *Ha.* 60 (1942), pp. 79–80. (Why not from *remora*, 'delay', the common noun : *re+mora* (cf. *repagula*, etc.)? Quantity alone makes Richardson's theory hard to accept.)

[2] 42 of these end pentameters.

SULCI: *EP* 2.10.33, *rate caeruleas picta sulcauimus undas*; *Aen.* 5.142, etc.

101 QUI SEMPER SPUMAS SEQUERIS, POMPILE, NITENTES: for the form of this line, cf. Auson. *Mos.* 107, *spumarum indiciis caperis, mustela, natantum*. It is clear that it is an etymological explanation of the name of the *pompilus*. Cf. Opp. 1.187, πομπῇ δ' ἐπεφήμισαν οὔνομα νηῶν.

POMPILE: cf. Appendix 6.

NITENTES: Birt (p. 29) devotes much attention to attacking the propriety of this word which, he claims, is suitable to the glassy hue of the *unda pura*, but not to the dazzling white of spume and spin-drift, which should be expressed by *canens* and *albescens*, and other allied words. He is in error, cf. *MF* 51, *dic age ... candida quo possint ora nitere modo*, which cannot refer to the desire of a lady to have a glassy complexion, and *T* 3.10.22, *et nitet inducto candida barba gelu*, which seems to have frost in mind rather than ice.

A lacuna must be indicated after this verse. The list from vv. 94–117 falls into two parts. The first part (vv. 94–101) corresponds in general to the list of deep-sea fishes given in Oppian 1.179 *et sq.* The second part (vv. 102–117) contains the names that are to be found in the lists of shore fishes given by Oppian (1.97 *et sq.*) (the *cantharus* is not mentioned by Oppian in his catalogue, but Aristotle (598 a 10) names it as a fish of the coastal waters). From *scopulorum fine moratur* (v. 102) and *saxatilis* (v. 109), it is obvious that our author meant the second part as a separate list of rock-fishes. I have given a detailed discussion in *Ovidiana*, p. 454 *et sq.*

Once the unity of the list from vv. 94–101 is established, Birt's proposal to transfer vv. 100–1, *post* v. 117, in order to harmonize the order in the *Halieutica* with that in Pliny (cf. Appendix 3), falls to the ground.

102 CERCYROS: the preservation of the Greek -*os* form is notable. In Greek the forms with υ and ου are both found, but only the latter for the fish-name (κέρκουρος).

SCOPULORUM FINE: taken by Pliny (32.152) as '*in scopulis*'; cf. *EP* 1.4.28, *qui uix Thessaliae fine timendus erat*.

MORATUR: it is very probable that *morantur* should be read here, but, as the context has been lost, one cannot be sure.

103 CANTHARUS: 'the Black Bream—*Sparus cantharus* (*L.*); *Cantharus lineatus* (*Gthr.*)', *DT* 100. He adds that it is, according to Xenocrates 9, a 'good table-fish', cf. Moreau 'peu recherché';

Schmid, p. 290, 'allein das *ingratus suco* passt auf diese Fische nicht'; Cotte, p. 103, says, 'Valenciennes compare sa chair, blanche et légère, a celle de Bars [viz. the Bass], ce qui ne paraît guère justifier, non plus, l'épithète *ingratus* d'Ovide.'

   SUCO: *sucus* sometimes in Latin means 'flavour', e.g. *(oua) suci melioris*, Hor. *sat.* 2.4.13, cf. Hor. *sat.* 2.8.28, Lucr. 3.223, etc. It seems best to take this meaning as being intended here. Neither ancient nor modern sources give any reason why the *cantharus* should be described as *ingratus suco*, and Birt emended (*et gratus*) to bring our text into line with εὔχυλος in Xenocrates 9, only to reject his emendation because Athenaeus shows ancient writers occasionally differed on such questions from Xenocrates. We must either presume that our author had a special personal dislike for the *cantharus*, or that he has remembered Ovid's line: *cantharidum sucos, dante parente, bibas* (*Ibis* 308), and confused the *cantharis*,[1] which was an insect, from which poison was prepared, with the *cantharus*. The word *sucus* is particularly suitable in the *Ibis* as it is especially used in describing the juices and extracts used in poisoning and witchcraft. It seems to me improbable that our author had some source lost to us which contradicted the common view of the taste of the *cantharus*, and he does not seem to have expressed personal opinions elsewhere about the fish. Hence I think it probable that he did mis-interpret *Ibis* 308, especially as so much imitation can be seen in our poem.

   TUM: cf. Appendix I.

   CONCOLOR: used four times by Ovid. The only previous known occurrence (cf. *ThLL* 4.81.5) is in Verg. *Aen.* 8.82.   *M* 11.500, *concolor est illis*, suggests our passage, cf. v. 124, *inf.* (*concolor* meaning *similis* is first found in Apuleius; cf. Axelson, *Eranos* 43 (1945), p. 31. One cannot say this meaning is required here; cf. next paragraph.)

   104 ORPHUS: I have adopted this spelling as representing the form used in Numenius and others (ὀρφός), rather than *orphos* representing the Attic ὀρφώς (cf. Athen. 315 a), because the Ms. *orphas* (cf. Prolegomena, p. 5) and the Doric forms of *echenais* and *polypus*, in our text, incline me to this opinion.[2] Was the *orphus* in fact *concolor cantharo*? It is identified with 'one of the two great Sea-perches'— *Serranus gigas*, or *Polyprion cernium* (*CV.*) by D'Arcy Thompson

---

[1] The form *cantharis* is also used for the fish, cf. *ThLL* and D'Arcy Thompson. The etymology is discussed by Cocco in *Studi Etruschi* 16 (1942), p. 387 *et sq.*, and referred to a 'Mediterranean' root KANTH, meaning 'curvature, roundness'.

[2] Cf. Pliny 32.152, *orphum*, which, as de Saint-Denis (*REA* 47 (1945), p. 290) points out, implies *orphus*. So too Vlitius. But the Mss. are very uncertain in Pliny (*orphim, morphym, morsum*).

(p. 187); and Cotte (p. 69) fixes on the latter 'avec beaucoup de réserves'. D'Arcy Thompson claims that both are 'much darker coloured' than the *cantharus*. I suppose one must see both to decide how important the discrepancy is.

CAERULEA: 'sea-blue', cf. Leumann, *Glotta* 34 (1955), p. 224.

RUBENS: this may be an etymological allusion to ἐρυθῖνος (cf. Oppian 1.97, ξανθοί τ' ἐρυθῖνοι; and vv. 98, 99, 101, 111?, 113?), or it may be a simple colour contrast with *caerulea*, as in v. 131, *nigrum niueo*.

UNDA: the singular may be used to avoid cacophony with *s* and the long *i* sounds.

105 INSIGNIS . . . NOTIS: cf. v. 113 and *M* 1.768, *radiis insigne*.

IULIS: this is a certain correction of Birt's for the Ms. ·*I·alis*. It is palaeographically convincing because of the frequent change of *a* and *u* (cf. Prolegomena, p. 5), and it is necessary because the order of the fish names set out in Pliny 32.152 requires the mention of the *iulus* between *erythinum* (v. 104) and *pictas mormyras* (v. 110) (for a general discussion of the order in Pliny 32.152, cf. Appendix 3). The adoption of this word here involves the rejection of Lachmann's reading of *iuli* in v. 95 for *milui* (cf. v. 95, *sup.*). The Ms. *milii* (v. 95) for *milui* makes one suspect that our *iulis* has lost a minim, and Pliny may preserve in his *iulum* the evidence for an *iulus* in our text instead of *iulis*—both forms are found in Greek (cf. *DT* 91). It is identified as 'one of the many species of Wrasse—especially the Rainbow Wrasse—*Coris iulis (Gthr.)*' (*DT*). It is gaily coloured, cf. Opp. 2.434, βαλιῇσιν ἰουλίσι, etc., and modern writers say it is the brightest of the Mediterranean, and does not yield to tropical fish. Hence *insignis*; and Birt's (p. 58) suggestion to read *notis ἀπὸ κοινοῦ* is not improbable (cf. βαλιός).

106 SUPER AURATA: editors generally take this as two words, and in view of such passages as *M* 4.240, *tumulumque super grauis addit harenae*, it seems reasonable to follow the example (*super* is hardly *in tmesi* in such uses, as they are fairly common).

SPARULUS: the Sea-bream, especially *Sparus annularis* (*L.*), *DT* 248, who adds 'as a fish known to all men, it is mostly mentioned only by name; . . . it feeds on green sea-weed by the shore (Opp. 1.109), a fact confirmed by various authors'. Schmid (p. 293) quotes Sucker (p. 22) for the colour: 'Färbung oberwärts goldig, unten silberig; ein schwarzer Ring umgibt die Schwanzwurzel.' D'Arcy Thompson quotes Cuvier: 'La couleur de ce sargue est d'une jaune presque doré sur le dos.' Cotte (p. 105) has some doubts.

CERUICE: a *plurale tantum* in older Latin: Maas, *ALL* 12 (1902), p. 501, and Löfstedt's *Syntactica*, i.31.

REFULGENS: evidently just *fulgens*. Cf. Schönwitz, pp. 46-9, p. 13. Cf. Verg. *Aen.* 1.402, *rosea ceruice refulsit*.

107 RUTILUS: cf. N. G. McCrea: 'Ovid's use of colour and colour terms':[1] '*Rutilus:* ...... a tone of high luminosity always. So of a jet of arterial blood [*M* 5.83], of the vivid reds of dawn [*M* 2.112] [*v. l.*], of the flashing light of flame [*M* 4.403; 12.294] and of lightning [*M* 11.436, etc.]. So too of lustrous reddish golden hair [*M* 2.319, 635; 6.715]. In the last instance, one should note that in l. 718 *flauescere* is used as its equivalent.' Cf. Wölfflin, *ALL* 12 (1902), p. 20, who shows that *rutilus* may be used to describe 'hochblond' hair.

PHAGER: *Pagrus vulgaris* (*CV.*), *Sparus pagrus* (*L.*), is suggested by *DT* 273. This is the Braize, or Becker, of British authors, but is liable to be confused in popular nomenclature with *Dentex macrophthalmus*, which is much redder (cf. Schmid, p. 293). The Ms. corruption is hard to explain, but the initial *ph* may have given *f*, taken as the *dasia* (cf. Havet, §1350), as E. W. Handley has suggested to me.

FULUI: the use of this word would make us suppose that the *red* rather than the *yellow* aspect of *rutilus* is stressed in this line.

SYNODONTES: *Dentex vulgaris* (*Cuv.*), *Sparus dentex* (*L.*)—a large and handsome fish of the sea bream family (*DT* 255). As for its colour, Athen. (322 b) quotes Numenius as terming it 'λευκή' but Epicharmus as 'ἐρυθροποίκιλος'. Sucker (quoted by Schmid, p. 294) says, 'Rücken blaugrau, die Seiten fallen etwas in Rötliche'; Schmid adds, 'oder sind, nach Moreau [iii.58], leicht goldiggelb. Rücken und Seiten zeigen schwarze Tupfen in unregelmässiger Verteilung. Dies könnte zu *fului*, rötlich-gelb, stimmen, auch zu ἐρυθροποίκιλος...'. But D'Arcy Thompson remarks that: '*fuluus* is ill-suited to any of the allied species'. Cotte (p. 102) seeks to solve the difficulty by remarking, 'mais, à l'état adulte, la teinte général devient plutôt rose', which is hardly satisfactory.[2] Oppian places it among the rocks and sands (1.170), but D'Arcy Thompson quotes Cuvier on p. 255, '... ayant pris l'hameçon à une grande profondeur...'.

---

[1] *Classical Studies in honour of Henry Drisler* (New York, 1894), p. 186.

[2] But de Saint-Denis, *REA* 47 (1945), p. 297: 'En effet, la Méditerranée possède deux espèces de dentés: le vulgaire, *dentale* des Italiens, qui est argenté; et la denté à gros yeux qui est rouge, *boucca rouga* à Nice.' First in Numenius, second Epicharmus and Ovid.

EX SE: the more usual form of the preposition is used instead of the literary *e* which would be cacophonous at the end of this line; (*ex* is normally used in common phrases by Ovid; cf. *ex me, ex re*, etc.).[1] Note the ending in three monosyllables.[2]

108 CONCIPIENS: Pliny 10.184, ... *mulier, non ex mari, uerum ex semet ipsa tantum conceperit* ... and, in Ovid, *A* 2.13.5, *ex me conceperat*.

CHANNE: Greek form, cf. Appendix 4, *inf.* D'Arcy Thompson: 'A Sea perch—*Serranus cabrilla*, or *S. scriba*' (p. 283). Cotte (p. 67) definitely commits himself to the former on the strength of the fishermen's usage in the modern languages. Schmid (p. 295) inclines to the latter. Its hermaphroditic nature is not mentioned by Oppian, who uses the masculine form χάννος. Aristotle (538 a 18; 760 a 9; 755 b 21) reported this fact; cf. also 567 a 26 (Pliny 9.56, and 9.166).

GEMINO NON FUNCTA PARENTE: this is my suggestion for the Ms. *gemino sibi fundata parente*: it merely explains *ex se concipiens*—'conceiving of itself, not making use of a twin (i.e. second) parent'. Haupt's reading is delightfully pointed, but the corruption to the Ms. version is improbable; Schenkl's reading is difficult in so far as it shifts the emphasis from the parenthood of the *channe* to her parentage. Birt's suggestions seem too clear to have been corrupted; I do not understand Curcio's conjecture. I assume an haplography of *no*; a dittography, by compensation, of *functa* as *functata* (the *ct* being ligatured and read as *d* (cf. Rand, p. 58)); and that the remaining *n* of *non* was read as *si* (the *nota* for *sibi*[3] (cf. *N.L.*, p. 123)).

GEMINO: this may refer either to 'a twin parent', the more natural meaning of the word (cf. Pacuv. *trag.* 173; Cic. *S. Rosc.* 118; Val. Flacc. 1.285), or 'a pair of parents', in the poetic licence which enabled *gemini* to be substituted for *ambo* or *duo*.

109 SAXATILIS: Haupt took this word to refer to some specific variety of fish, and he seems to be correct. *saxatilis* is used as the name of a species in the following passages: *Anth. Lat.* 390.17, and Ambr. *hex.* 5.10.26, *ille sinus maris cephalos alit, lupos ille, ille saxatiles,*

---

[1] Cf. Axelson, *Unpoetische Wörter*, p. 120. Löwe's programme, which was inaccessible to Axelson, states: (1) (a) *ex* before monosyllables (but *e quis*); (b) other words: *e* before *g, l, q, s*; otherwise variation; but, of course, (2) always *ex* before vowels and *h*.

[2] Not very infrequent in Ovid. A full list of occurrences is given in [F.] B. Eschenburg's *Metrische Untersuchungen ueber die Aechtheit der Heroides des Ovids* (Lübeck, 1874), on p. 9.

[3] If Wakefield's *sibi* for the *si* of OQ at Lucr. 3.183 is correct, there is further evidence for this rare *nota*.

lucustas alius. Papendick (p. 29) shows that the glossaries give '*φυκίδες*: *saxatiles*' and holds this view. The *saxatiles* would then seem to be some of the family of wrasses (rock fishes with small mouths), perhaps the *Labrus turdus* (*L.*), which is of a greenish colour; cf. notes on v. 114.

Birt also came to this identification, but considers (pp. 108–9) that *saxatilis* is a generic name for the rock fishes, and holds that the *turdus* is meant κατ' ἐξοχήν. Such allusiveness seems to be out of place in a didactic poem, but we must admit that Pliny and Columella use *saxatilis* as a generic name only.[1] Schmid (p. 296) holds that this verse refers to the *faber* (or John Dory, cf. *DT* 281) mentioned in the next verse, claiming that 'nur *paruo ore* scheint nicht zuzutreffen'. This objection is fatal to his theory, as modern writers comment on the size of the John Dory's mouth—cf. Jordan (ii. 249), 'the mouth (is) large'; and Norman (p. 117), 'the John Dory with its large . . . mouth'.

110   The form μορμύλος is found in Oppian 1.100 and Athen. 313 e. For the confusion of λ and ρ, cf. Schwyzer, *Griechische Grammatik*, i.213. Cotte derives the word from the root of μορμύρω (p. 106). I have not found any other occurrence of *mormyr*, save Pliny's quotation from here. Cf. Appendix 6.

111   (AURI) . . . DECUS: cf. Hor. *ep.* 5.7, *purpurae decus*. Cf. ἀγλαΐη, Opp. 1.169.

TUM: cf. Appendix 1.

CORPORIS UMBRAE (LIUENTIS): a variation, *metri gratia*, for the ablative, vv. 95, 109, etc.

UMBRAE: 'The Maigre—*Sciaena aquila (Cuv.)*—and its close allies', *DT* 241. Cf. Varro, *ling.* 5.77, *alia a coloribus, ut . . . umbra.*

112   LIUENTIS: well used of a shadowy hue; cf. the British pearls, Tac. *Agr.* 12.6, 'gris bleuâtre', André, p. 173.

RAPIDI LUPI: (cf. vv. 23–6, 39–42). Schmid (p. 265) quotes from Brehm (p. 40) an account parallel to that in vv. 39–42. Cf. *DT* 140.

113   QUIN: cf. Appendix 1.

LAUDE CAUDAE: cf. *laude pedum . . . praestantior esset, M* 10.563.

O. Skutsch suggests that *nigrore* should be read for *quin laude.* This reading would give the etymology[2] of *melanurus*, and rid the text of the awkward *quin. nigrore* would match very well *ardens auratis . . . notis* (113–4) and *uirentes* (114). The omission of a conjunction would be in the author's style, cf. Appendix 1. The

---

[1] Plin. 9.57, etc., Colum. 8.16.8.
[2] Cf. references under *Etymologies* in *Index Verborum et Rerum*, and the parallel *candore* in v. 124.

repetition of sound in *laude* . . . *caudae* is hardly significant evidence of corruption.

ARDENS: 'shining'. So used, according to the *ThLL* (2.487.46), by the following poets: Vergil, Lucan, Homerus Latinus, Statius, Valerius Flaccus, Silius, and later authors.

114 MURENA: cf. vv. 27–30 and 43–5, *sup.* (for spelling, cf. Keller, *Antike Tierwelt*, ii.363, Müller, *Lucilius*, p. 221). *ferox* (v. 27) may refer to its two rows of great teeth, above and below (cf. Aelian 9.40) mentioned by D'Arcy Thompson (p. 162), and more especially alludes to what Schmid (p. 268) describes: 'Gefangene kämpfen wütend . . . und bringen ungeschickten Fischern gefährliche Wunden bei'.

MERULAE: Greek Κόσσυφοι: 'One of the many species of Labridae or Wrasses, e.g. *Labrus merula* (L.)', *DT* 128; Schmid (p. 301) says: 'Ohne Zweifel *Labrus merula*, oder *livens* (Linn.).'

115 Vlitius' suggestion that *genti* should be read in this line seems to have been adopted independently by Vollmer from a consideration of the Ms. which shows *gentei* (very probably representing *gente* written in error, with the correct termination added), changed to *gentes*—from the influence of *suae*. The reading of Sannazaro is awkward and hardly deserving of adoption.

CANCER: most editors have changed this word to *gonger* or *conger*, because Aristotle (591 a 17) says that conger eels are especially accustomed to eat each other. Lenz (in his edition) remarks that this is not quite what is stated in our text. I think that Plin. 9.99, *cancri . . . demicant inter se ut arietes, aduersis cornibus incursantes,* justifies the retention of the Ms. reading.

Vlitius' argument in favour of the *cancer*—'praesertim cum scorpius sequatur' is hardly valid, for the *scorpios* is one of the class *pareioplitae* which have 'mailed cheek-bones' but normal skins elsewhere (Jordan, ii.433).

cancer: a Crab,[1] especially the common edible crab: *Cancer pagurus* (L.), *DT* 105.

INMITIS . . . PER UULNERA is, as Birt says (p. 113), *constructa . . . inelegantissime*, but may be defended from *Ep.* 12.41, *Martis erant tauri plus quam per cornua saeui*. Heinsius bracketed this line with a cryptic '[Hoc] distichon Ouidanae non uidetur esse uenae'; but modern editors, following Bentley, have removed the brackets. Cf. Appendix 2.

---

[1] *cancer*, at Pliny 9.99 and here, may mean the 'hermit crab', cf. Oppian 1.335. There is some evidence for such confusion of καρκίνος and καρκινάς, contrast Opp. *Cyn.* 2.286 with Ar. 611 b 21 (Pliny 8.97).

116 SCORPIOS: the Ms. *scorpio* may be explained as assimilation to the more familiar form. This fish is identified as the 'Bullhead or Fatherlasher' (the German 'Drachenkopf'), scientifically known as the *Scorpaena*, of which there are two varieties mentioned in Athen. 320 e by Hicesius: the former πελάγιος (*Sc. scrofa*) and the latter τεναγώδης (*Sc. porcus*), καὶ ὁ μὲν πελάγιος πυρρός, ὁ δ᾽ ἕτερος μελανίζων. One must assume that the first is intended here. It is described by D'Arcy Thompson (p. 245) as a 'small but formidable-looking fish with a great head armed with sharp spines, which give an angry wound'. In fact it would seem that it is the twelve dorsal spines which have the poisonous properties,[1] but the names 'Bullhead' and 'Drachenkopf' show that it is the head of the animal which captures the imagination, and our poet was hardly conscious of the distinction between the head and the spines just behind it.

It has been proposed to read *captus* on the ground that *nociturus* implies something in the future, but the parallel passage in Ausonius, *Mos.* 89, *et nullo spinae nociturus acumine rhedo*, shows just the same construction with a vague unexpressed protasis. Cf. Stolz-Schmalz, p. 606, and Sil. 17.651, *salue inuicte parens, non concessure Quirino laudibus, ac meritis non concessure Camillo!* Cf. also: *nulla nocituro grauis suco tumescat herba*, Sen. *Herc. F.* 935. Birt's *diro* for *duro*[2] on the grounds that the words were constantly confused by scribes, and that *dirus* is more suitable to the pain of a poisoned wound is plausible, and may be supported by such phrases as *M* 3.694, *diris . . . tormentis* and *diris cruciatibus*, *M* 9.179. However, on consideration of such uses as *Aen.* 5.436, *duro crepitant sub uulnere malae*, it would seem best to leave the text stand, as it is a matter which could be settled only with the aid of a detailed knowledge of the author's use of the two words: and his attitude to imitation is such that we must allow for the influence of other poets.

117 AESTIUO . . . SIDERE: 'in summer', cf. *brumali sidere*, 'in winter', *EP* 2.4.25; poetic diction (cf. Bednara, *ALL* 14 (1906), p. 594[3], but cf. Mela 1.52, *aestiuo sidere*. For an explanation of the corruption of *aestiuo* to *stiuo*, cf. O. Prinz, *Glotta* 26 (1938), p. 104 *et sq.*).

GLAUCUS: 'An oft-mentioned fish name, but, like many such, impossible to identify', *DT* 48. A fish of the rocks and sands according to Oppian (1.170), but pelagic according to Aristotle (598 a 13),

---

[1] Cf. Jordan ii.433.

[2] *duro* is a suitable word since the head of the *scorpios* has 'mailed cheek-bones' and this fact may have been in the author's mind. Cf. note on *cancer*, v. 115.

[3] No doubt, if any particular *sidus* is intended, *Sirius* is in mind; cf. Opp. (1.152; 3.48), Pliny (9.133, etc.), Ar. (599 b 31).

who records (599 b 32) its aestivation. De Saint-Denis (*REA* 47
(1945), p. 298) identifies it with Aristotle's γαλεός (565 b 24),
Squalus glaucus, (*L.*), 'peau bleue', from the statement in Opp. 1.747
—but does it aestivate?[1]

118 AT CONTRA: cf. Appendix 1. As the introduction to the
rock-fishes has been lost in the lacuna after v. 101, I think that here
the contrast is not between the deep sea and the weed-covered sand,
as most editors have assumed, but rather between the rocks, and the
weeds on the sandy shore. I set out a comparison of the catalogue of
fishes in the weeds with the information in Oppian:

Fishes in our text	Placed by Oppian in:	
vv. 119 et sq.		
scarus	weedy rocks	(1.134)
mena	weedy beach	(1.108)
lamiros	——	
smaris	weedy beach	(1.109)
chromis	?river mouths	(1.112)
mullus	mud	(1.105)
soleae	sand	(1.99)
passer	——	
rhombus	mud	(1.105)
lepores	——	
ranae	——	
gobius	rocks and sands	(1.174)
lolligo	——	
caris	rocks	(1.281)
asellus	gulfs of the sea	(1.151)
acipenser	——	

This makes one suspect that our text has been mutilated after
v. 120.

HERBOSA . . . HARENA: cf. Auson. *Mos.* 85, *squameus herbosas capito
inter lucet harenas*.

LUXANTUR—Ms. *laxantur*: this word (despite the defence of
Vlitius who sees in it evidence of the authorship of Grattius, and
compares Gratt. 56, *laxare retia* (does he mean 'dispersed'?)) seems
incapable of a clear interpretation. Palaeographically (cf. Prolegomena, p. 5) the simplest restoration is Haupt's *luxantur*. This
word is found in use only at Plaut. *Pseud.* 1107. Nonius (335.37) has
this passage, and Festus had to explain (p. 120 M) our verb.
laetantur is supported by similar expressions in use elsewhere:

---

[1] Norman (p. 244) claims that: 'aestivation . . . does not occur among the
inhabitants of the sea, but among fresh water fishes.' If this is so, Aristotle was
mistaken in his statements that the *glaucus* aestivates and is a pelagic fish.

7—H.

v. 94, *sup.*, *gaudent pelago*; Oppian 1.383, γάνυνται; 3.415, τέρπονται; Ar. (Athen. 315 a), χαίρει δὲ πρόσγειος . . . ὧν. *mollis alga*, which is mentioned *supra*, v. 91, seems to lend some counter-support to *luxantur*. It is very hard to decide.

119 UT: cf. Appendix 1.

SCARUS: its place at the head of the class here has been compared with Pliny's *nunc principatus scaro datur* (9.62). This is hardly more than a coincidence, but cf. Papendick, p. 15.

EPASTAS: this is a 'hapax legomenon', and it seems that the line has been influenced to some extent by passages in Ovid: *RA* 740, *hic uomit epotas dira Charybdis aquas*, and *A* 3.5.18, *et iterum pasto pascitur ante cibo*. *epastas* is an anomalous form if used in the passive construction, according to Birt (p. 36), but the confusion of such medio-passive past participles is notorious (cf. *emersus*, v. 36, and Ovid's use of *pasto*, *A* 3.5.18, and *epotas*, *RA* 740 (contrast the common *bene potus*, etc.)) and should be sufficient justification.

SOLUS QUI: inversion by the ' *Troiae qui* rule'; contrast Pliny 9.62, *qui solus . . . dicitur ruminare*; Cic. *har. resp.* 14, etc.

RUMINAT: on *e* for *a*, cf. Prolegomena, p. 5.

ESCAS: means no more than 'food' in our text here, in contrast to vv. 11 and 38, where it means 'bait'.

120 FECUNDUMQUE GENUS MENAE: *genus* (a race) with a plural genitive tended naturally to refer to the *genus* as a whole (e.g. *genus . . . Marcellorum*, Cic. *Verr.* 3.51), composed of its members, but with a singular genitive it tended to refer to the race as a descendant of some ancestor (e.g. *Caesaris . . . genus*, *Eleg. in Maecen.* 2.30; very similar is *fecundum est . . . Cancri genus*, Manil. 2.236). Yet the slightly different meaning of *genus* like our 'kind' naturally took a singular genitive in such phrases as *genus est animalis*, Colum. *arb.* 15; *nouumque id genus imperii uisum est*, Cic. *rep.* 2.56, etc., where the reference is to the members rather than any *auctor* or ancestor. Thus it would appear to be possible to read *menae* as a singular genitive to balance the other singular nouns in the line.

Yet, on examining Sil. 14.95 (*ThLL* 6.1889.68 hesitates on this passage),

> *Pyrrhus origo dabat stimulos proauique superbum*
> *Aeacidae genus atque aeternus carmine Achilles,*

(where it seems very awkward to take *Aeacidae* as a singular) and Vergil's *dirum tiniae genus* (*Geo.* 4.246) (where the plural is convincingly supported by *ignauom fucos pecus* (*Geo.* 4.168)), I have somewhat doubtfully decided in favour of taking *genus* as being in apposition to *menae* (nom. pl.) in our passage.

MENAE: the usual form in the Mss. according to the *ThLL*; preferred by L. Müller (*Lucilius*, p. 242), cf. *supra*, on the form *murena* (v. 114).

DT 247 takes *lamirosque smarisque* as being in apposition to *fecundumque genus menae*.

121 INMUNDA CHROMIS: D'Arcy Thompson (p. 292) falls into confusion in dealing with this fish, for he overlooks the fact that Pliny 32.153 is a quotation of this passage, and makes the revealing observation that '*Immunda chromis* . . . is, in all probability, the same as Pliny's fish'.

An extraordinary difficulty is to discover how Pliny read our text to understand that it was the *chromis* that built nests in the water, particularly as he had stated[1] (9.81) that the *phycis* alone did so. The simplest solution of the difficulty about Pliny's quotation is to suppose with de Saint-Denis (*RPh* III, 18 (1944), p. 157): 'Il est évident que, dans ces deux vers Ovide énumère trois poissons: 1° *chromis*; 2° *salpa*; 3° un poisson constructeur de nids, désigné par une périphrase' (so Haupt, p. xxi); 'et qu'une lecture trop rapide de ces vers a causé l'erreur de Pline. . . .' The error attributed to Pliny is not too unlikely in view of the other instances that de Saint-Denis collects in his article (cf. also Münzer, p. 81). Yet I do not believe that in such a catalogue a name would be designated by a periphrasis unless it could not be made to scan in the verse. I hold that we should rather believe that a line has fallen out of the text.

Hartel, however, suggests that Pliny 32.153 should read *eum qui nidificet in aquis*, and that *chromis* is a gloss (*ZöG* 17(1866), p. 335). We have still to assume that the writer of the gloss made the error which Hartel does not wish to attribute to Pliny. One curious point that seems to have been overlooked and rather tells in favour of Hartel's theory is that the text of Pliny (32.153) makes *chromis* masculine—(yet this is the usual gender in Greek).

Schmid's theory that *inmunda* refers to the colour of the *Sciaena aquila* seems unlikely (p. 305).

MERITO UILISSIMA SALPA: the Saupe—*Box salpa* (*CV.*) disliked as food—Archestratus (Athen. 321 e), σάλπην δὲ κακὸν μὲν ἔγωγε ἰχθὺν εἰς ἀεὶ κρίνω (*DT* 224), Pliny 9.68, *alii alibi pisces principatum optineant . . . circa Ebusum salpa*, *obscaenus alibi*. . . . The epithet *uilissima* may have reference to more than the flavour of the *salpa*. Cf. Aristotle 534 a 16, δελεάζεται . . . τῇ κόπρῳ and 591 a 15;

---

[1] And this was Aristotle's view, cf. 607 b 19.

Epicharmus (Athen. 321 d), σκατοφάγοι σάλπαι βδελυχραί and the Provençal name 'manjo-merdo' (Cotte, p. 111).

There is only one apparent way to take the text without assuming that Pliny has been guilty of the gravest carelessness, and that is to presume that he understood the text to identify the *chromis* with the *salpa*, and read 'the filthy *chromis*—the meritedly most despised *salpa* and (which) imitates the sweet nests of the birds in the waves'. But Aristotle mentions the fish together without any indication of identity, 534 a 9.

Although *inmunda*[1] seems rather to suggest the feeding of the *salpa*, and give *merito* a reason, the use of *merito* to express identity in the sense *uere* is late, and never occurs in this epexegetic form (*ThLL* 8.824.45). Then we must assume that Pliny has quoted either from memory or inaccurate notes.

UILISSIMA SALPA: ancient theory disliked such endings in the same vowel, but exceptions were allowed for deliberate effect. Cf. Norden, p. 405 *et sq.* (esp. p. 407, footnote 3), who quotes *Geo.* 3.219, *pascitur in magna Sila formosa iuuenca*. Cf. also Platnauer, p. 40.

122 DULCES: it has been suggested that *phycis* should be read here, since Aristotle (607 b 19) and Pliny (9.81) are so definite that of all fishes only the *phycis* built nests in the sea. Yet, as Pliny has related this of the *chromis* when he excerpted the information, it seems improbable that *phycis* was in his text. If our identification of *saxatilis* as φυκίς is correct there is a further reason for refusing to read *phycis* here (cf. notes on v. 109). Finally, the phrase *dulces nidos* strongly recalls the other imitations of Vergil in our text (cf. Appendix 5). As the statement cannot refer to the *salpa*, it seems that we must assume a lacuna in the text as suggested by Pantagathus and Gesner.

DULCES NIDOS: imitated, it would appear, from *Aen.* 5.214 (cf. *Geo.* 1.414); cf. *dulcis nidi* (Sil. 11.467).

123 SQUAMAS: as there is no gap left in A it seems fair to conclude that the error is the result of haplography, and Birt's *squatina et* might claim our attention,[2] yet the parallel from Pliny 9.66[3] may

---

[1] Or is it influenced by *obscaenus*, Pliny 9.68?

[2] The *squatus* seems to be the Greek ῥίνη, and also to be the same fish as the *squatina* (cf. *DT* 221; de Saint-Denis, *Vocabulaire* ..., p. 108). Then we must conclude that it was a deep-sea fish and unsuited to this list of fishes which seem rather to be inshore fishes, cf. v. 118, *sup*. Cf. Opp. 1.381, where the ῥίνη is found among the Sea-monsters. The *squatus* may thus be identified with the Monk or Angel Fish (*Squalus squatina* (*L.*)).

[3] *mullum expirantem uersicolori quadam et numerosa uarietate spectari proceres gulae narrant, rubentium squamarum multiplici mutatione pallescentem* ...; cf. also Sen. *nat.* 3.18.5 for ideas.

decide us in favour of *squamas*. The apocryphal *squalus* has no firm
authority (cf. Forcellini, *s.v.*), but there might be something in
favour of *squatus et.*

TENUI . . . SANGUINE: hardly in contrast to the *crassus sanguis*[1] of
other animals; probably merely conventional epithet (cf. v. 19,
sup.).

SQUAMAS . . . SUFFUSUS: cf. *rubra suffusus lumina flamma, M* 11.368;
as in many such cases, one can hardly say whether the accusative is
governed by the middle voice, or whether it is felt as an accusative
of respect.[2]

124 CONCOLOR: cf. on v. 103.

125 ADRIACO MIRANDUS LITORE: cf. Juv. 4.39, *incidit* Adriaci
spatium admirabile *rhombi*, and Pliny 9.168–9, *eadem aquatilium
genera aliubi atque aliubi meliora ut . . . rhombus Rauennae.* There is no
reason to take the ablatives as being other than locative. Cf. v. 134,
inf., v. 87, *sup.*

126 TUM: the Ms. has *tunc*, a form which is not guaranteed by
the metre in any passage of enumeration in the Latin poets of
classical times (Housman ad Manil. 2.213). Cf. Appendix 1. The
parasitic *c*, no doubt, arose from the following *l*, cf. *coci* for *loci*, v. 85.

LEPORES: there is no reason to adopt the obviously corrupt
readings of Pliny 32.152. The *lepus* is probably the Sea-Hare,
Aplysia depilans (*L.*), described (*DT* 142) as 'a kind of sea-slug with
large ear-like tentacles'. De Saint-Denis (*REA* 47 (1945), p. 300)
argues plausibly for this identification.

LATI: evidently what Pliny read (cf. 32.152).

MOLLES TERGORE: this is probably to be explained by Ar.
695 b 14 (cf. 696 a 27), where he explains that the Angler is an
exception to the general rule that fishes have either long, slender,
hard tails, or short, broad, fleshy ones, διὰ γὰρ τὸ μὴ σαρκῶδες εἶναι
τὸ πλάτος αὐτῶν τὸ ἐμπρόσθιον, ὅσον ἀφήρηται σαρκῶδες πρὸς τὸ
ὄπισθεν αὐτὸ ἔθηκεν ἡ φύσις καὶ τὴν οὐράν. (Schmid's 'Der Körper ist
nackt (Günther, S. 333), daher *molles tergore*' (p. 315) does not seem
to be so plausible. Cf. Oppian 2.86, μαλθακὸς ἰχθύς.) This seems to
involve taking *tergus* in the sense of 'back' (τὸ ὄπισθεν) as applied to
the fish's tail, as the sense 'skin' (cf. v. 64), does not seem to suit
here; cf. v. 95, *sup.* (cf. Birt, p. 123).

RANAE: the Angler, or Sea-frog (*Lophius piscatorius*), *DT* 28.

127 It seems futile to endeavour to reconstruct the gap here.

130 LUBRICUS: in view of the following remarks I take this word

---

[1] Lucan. 6.186, etc.
[2] Cf. Seneca *nat.* (3.18.1), *rubor primum, deinde pallor subfunditur.*

to agree with a noun in the lacuna—if it is not a translation of the fish name ὄλισθος, which Mair identifies with the *Silurus glanis*,[1] the Sheatfish (on Oppian 1.113).

GOBIUS: the Goby, of which Schmid (p. 315) claims there are nearly 300 varieties known. Housman (in Postgate's *Corpus*) identified our *gobius* with the κωβιός of Oppian, and emended the text to read *spina nocuus non gobius una*, because Oppian's fish has sharp spines and is poisonous. This does not seem to be required if we identify with the gobies described by Cuvier (quoted by Mair on Opp. 2.458): 'the simple rays of the Gobies are flexible and cannot wound'. This suits the text in the Ms. It seems less probable that *lubricus* refers to the flexible rays; it would be most suitable for describing a smooth-skinned eel-like fish. *gobius* seems to be a loan word from the Greek κωβιός, and the form *cobius* was used in Latin by some authors (cf. *ThLL* 6.2125.35), but the Mss. tend to supplant it with the form in *g*. Usage seems to have varied (cf. Stolz-Schmalz, p. 125).

NOCUUS seems to be attested definitely in this passage only (on Mart. 3.99.3, cf. Heraeus *ad loc.*; Scrib. Larg. 114 is very doubtful). It is clearly required by the metre, and seems to show something of the tendency that we have noticed in *non sana*, v. 51, *sup.* Any poet could easily think of the form by inversion from *innocuus* (Bréal, *MSL* 18 (1914), p. 177, argues that the form is analogous to *uacuus*, cf. *uaciuus*, *nociuus*).

It seems that the scribe left a gap of one line in the Ms. here, but on second thoughts extended the shaft of his initial letter (in *Lubricus*) to obscure the interval.

131 NIGRUM NIUEO: cf. *caeruleaque rubens*, v. 104.

UIRUS: cf. Hor. *sat.* 1.4.100, *nigrae sucus lolliginis* (by hypallage for *niger sucus lolliginis*). *niveus* is a hyperbole, Cotte, p. 188.

132 DURI SUES: there seems to be nothing to enable this fish to be identified. D'Arcy Thompson (p. 272) treats Oppian's ὕαινα as 'a fierce and monstrous, but unknown, fish', which seems to tally with *duri*. Schmid says 'Vielleicht *Silurus glanis*, der Wels', and sees *durus* as relating to the flesh (English: the Sheatfish). Cotte (p. 152) makes it the *orbis*—poisson lune—sunfish: '*Orthagoriscus mola*, Bl., devenu *Mola mola*.' The most ambitious treatment of the subject is given by Andrews in *TAPhA* 79 (1948), p. 232 *et sq.* He informs us that Ovid describes the *sus*, or 'pig fish' as having a hard skin! (p. 238); and connects this with the account given by Aristotle (Athen. 305 d) of the 'boar-fish', which, he suggests, may be the

---

[1] However, cf. on *sues*, v. 132, *inf.*

'file-fish' (*Balistes capriscus*). The paper seems to be merely a mass of elaborate guess-work.

SINUOSAQUE CARIS: 'A small crustacean, other than Crab or Lobster, including the "hunchbacks" or prawns . . .', and the 'hunchbacks or prawns' seem to be the best interpretation here in view of the word *sinuosa*, which seems fairly to render the Greek κυφός, which is constantly used to describe them (Eubul. *ap.* Athen. 106 a, καρίδες τε τῶν κυφῶν Philoxen., *ibid.* 147 b, καρίδες αἱ κυφαί, etc.; the words κυρτός and καμπύλος are also used) (*DT* 103).

133 DEFORMI: Ovid seems to have been fond of this word, for he uses it not infrequently, and has it in a sense not found in any other author in *F* 2.554, where it translates the Greek ἄμορφος.

ASELLUS[1]: a fish of the Cod family—especially the Hake, *Gadus merluccius* (*L.*), *DT* 182. Cotte objects to Varro's statement (*ling.* 5.77) that the fish was named for its colour, on the ground that the different species have different colours (p. 130). It was a valued fish—Varro, *Men.* 403—and hence *tam deformi non dignus nomine*. What was *deformis* about the name *asellus* to the Romans? Housman has already shown (*CQ* 24 (1930), p. 11 *et sq.*) that the poets who have any pretensions to elevation of style all avoid the word *asinus* for 'ass', and substitute *asellus* (the fish seems never to be known as *asinus*, cf. Papendick, p. 17). It seems that here, as is often the case with euphemisms, the euphemistic force of *asellus* has been lost, and our author reacts to it just as he would to *asinus*, which carried an *imago*, as the *ThLL* (2.794.37) says, 'maxime de stultitia, pigritia, obstinatione, uilitate, castigatione, sim.' Axelson, *Unpoetische Wörter*, pp. 44–5, remarks that similarly Vergil and Ovid strongly prefer *capella* to *capra*, and attributes to *asinus* 'einen unfeinen Klang'.

There are many passages where *asellus* is used in a *sensus obscaenus*, and it might be argued that the author is making an allusion to this. If this is the case it is rather strange, as the tone of the work is so serious in other respects. Cf. however, *F* 6.346, 1.391; *Priap.* 52.9; Sen. *Oed.* 429; Lact. *inst.* 1.21.30; Min. Fel. 9.3; Phaedr. 1.29.7; Lampr. *Commod.* 10.9; Cat. 97.10; Apul. *met.* 10.19–22; Juv. 11.97 (cf. 6.334); and, most remarkable of all, with a direct allusion to the fish, Petronius 24, *haec* [sc. *mentula*] . . . *belle cras in promulside libidinis nostrae militabit; hodie enim post asellum diaria non sumo.*[2] Cf. also J. Carcopino, *Daily Life in Ancient Rome* (1956), p. 253, and references given on p. 316.

[1] Greek ὄνος—D'Arcy Thompson; ὀνίσκος—Cass. Felix 28·(p. 44.17R). Cf. Mair, *Oppian*, etc., Intro. lxiii; Papendick, p. 17.
[2] Surely the Romans were not reminded of *assellari* (=*cacare*), cf. O. Keller, *Gram. Aufs.*, p. 179 ('Plin. Val. Veget.')?

For the notion of a *uox deformis*, cf. Cic. *rep.* 3. *fr.* 4, *Sardana*pallus [cf. φαλλός] *ille uitiis multo quam nomine ipso deformior*, and Quint. *decl.* 344 (pp. 358.16) (of the *meretrix*).

134 TUQUE: possibly meant as a concluding formula to the list, as Birt suggests; cf. v. 100.

PEREGRINIS . . . UNDIS: cf. *Adriaco litore* (v. 125) for the locative sense —one consequently wonders whether *litus* should there be taken as in v. 87 ('inshore waters'), for, if it is argued that the *rhombus* would not be considered *mirandus* until he was caught, then the *nobilitas* of the *acipenser* would be similarly devoid of admirers in the waves. So, all in all, *Adriaco litore* may be fairly translated 'off the Adriatic coast'.

ACIPENSER: the Sturgeon—*Acipenser sturio* (*L.*). This fish is the commonest variety of the Sturgeon in the Western Mediterranean, and it is quite possible that the author was thinking of some other variety—perhaps the *helops*—when he talks of its fine quality in foreign waters. Pliny (9.60) seems also to be confused when he says that he does not see why it is not popular now-a-days, particularly on account of its scarcity (implying that it did not taste so well as the preference of the *antiqui* implied), and adds that some thought it was the *helops*. When he read our text, however, he saw it claimed that the *helops* was *nostris incognitus undis*—so it could not be the *acipenser* (32.153). Cicero seems[1] to have been doubtful about its identity: *fat. frg.* 5, . . . *est piscis, ut ferunt, in primis nobilis.* Cf. v. 96, *sup.*; *DT* 7.

NOBILIS: cf. Pliny 9.27, *apud antiquos piscium nobilissimus habitus acipenser*, and Cicero quoted at the end of the preceding paragraph.

[1] It may be a device to disclaim expert knowledge, or to emphasize the simple tastes of the *antiqui*!

Conjunctions

(a) *Connexion in the Catalogue*

The particles used to connect the names of fishes in the catalogue
are most diversified. They are set out below (a double bar—‖—
denotes lack of any particle).

Catalogue of Pelagii, *vv. 94–100*
   que . . . que . . . ‖ . . . et . . . et . . . ac . . . et . . . ‖ . . . que.
The variation in our passage may well be paralleled from Verg.
Aen. 6.286 *et sq.*, *Centauri . . . Scylla*eque . . . et . . . *Briareus* . . . ac
*belua Lernae, . . . flammis*que *armata Chimaera*, Gorgones, *Harpiae*que,
et *forma tricorporis umbrae*, where *que, et, ac,* and the lack of particle,
are all to be seen.[1]

The catalogue of Saxatiles, *vv. 102–17*
   Here the skeleton is even more diverse:

que . . . ‖ . . .
tum . . . que . . . que . . . (anaphora) . . . et . . . et . . . et . . . et . . .
tum . . . et . . . et . . . et . . .
tum . . . que . . . que . . . . que . . .
quin . . . et . . . que . . . que . . . et . . . ac . . .

It may be remarked that *ac* rather suitably comes at the end of the
list. I have set out the *tum*'s as though they divided the names into
groups, and led up to the climax of *quin*. It is hard to say whether
such was the intention of the poet, or whether he just used *tum* as
a variety of *et* which began with a consonant (the italicized cases
are required by the metre).

TUM: when this word is used in enumeration, it has the force of
adding a fresh item in a certain progression. Thus, when Plautus
says *in Epidamnieis uoluptarii atque potatores . . . tum sycophantae . . .
in urbe hac habitant* (*Men.* 259), the addition of a fresh point is marked
by *tum* (as the *Lexicon Plautinum*, ii.809, remarks, 'addit aliquid noui').
Cicero often uses a series of *tum*'s to denote that things happen at

---

[1] The variation of copulative conjunctions in Tacitus and others is well discussed
in Kienzle, *Kopulativpartikeln*, p. 21 *et sq.*

different times (cf. *de oratore* 3.203; *rep.* 2.2); even in *nat. deor.* 3.43, *Acheron Cocytus Pyriphlegethon tum Charon tum Cerberus di putandi*, there is a change of class when we come to the items introduced with *tum*. So, even in poetic usages, e.g. Stat. *Theb.* 9.127, *Phocea tum Cydona Tanagreumque Phalanthum atque Erycem . . . figit*—where the latter warriors were slain after the first—*Aen.* 8.328, *tum manus . . . uenere . . . tum reges . . .*; *buc.* 2.45, *lilia . . . ecce ferunt Nymphae . . . Nais . . . narcissum et florem iungit . . . anethi, . . . tum . . . pingit uaccinia calta*, we seem always to have the notion of progression.

It is hard to see what the force of *tum* can be in our text. We can hardly imagine the fishes passing in some sort of a review. As most of the cases are required by the metre, it may be that *tum* is simply substituted for *et* where the preceding syllable could not be elided. In v. 126 the balance of the line may have caused the first example where the metre does not require the form; but v. 109 is not so to be explained.

QUIN: this use can hardly be defended unless we assume that it is intended to introduce all the fish before v. 117 as a climax to end the list. It seems too emphatic to introduce the *melanurus* alone. Cf. in Vergil's catalogue *Aen.* 7.750, *quin et Marruuia uenit de gente sacerdos*, where the verb is present, and the force of *sacerdos* [*ad bellum*] *uenit* accounts for the use of *quin*. I have not found any example of the use of *quin* without a verb save *Aen.* 7.321; cf. on v. 75, *sup.*

Macrobius (5.15.14–15) sees in Vergil's use of *tum* and *quin* a device to avoid the monotony of δέ and τε in Homer's catalogue.

Catalogue of Herbiuores, *vv. 118–34*

The co-ordinate conjunctions here do not seem to call for any special remark, except in the case of the omission of the conjunction before *merito* (v. 121), which is a word that often implies a particular connexion with the preceding item; but evidently such is not intended here (yet cf. *supra* on v. 121). *tum* (v. 126, *altero loco*) is required by the metre. The occasional omission of a copulative conjunction seems to be as old as Ennius[1]: *Ann.* 128, *libaque fictores, Argeos et tutulatos*; cf. Lucr. 4.1197, etc., Manil. 5.6, and Vergil *Aen.* 6.286 already quoted in this Appendix. Ehwald (cf. Lenz, *Sokrates* 76 (1922), p. 144) proposed to read 95, *hippuri* ⟨*et*⟩; 121, *merito* ⟨*et*⟩; 124, *soleae* ⟨*et*⟩; and he posits lacunae at vv. 98 and 102, as he believed Ovid was the author, and realized that he would have added the conjunctions. These are improbable suggestions[2].

[1] Colloquial, according to Tidner, p. 29; cf. p. 52 *et sq.*, esp. p. 55.
[2] Cf. *pugnant*, v. 4, and section (f) of this Appendix.

(b) *Other Co-ordinate Conjunctions*

The use of the rather prosaic *at contra* in vv. 31, 118 may be remarked.

AC: for the avoidance of this word in the 'lyrisch-elegische Stil' but the greater tolerance afforded to it in the 'episch-didaktische Stil', cf. Axelson, *Unpoetische Wörter*, pp. 82–3.[1] There are two cases in the text (vv. 97; 117).

ATQUE: the final syllable of the word is normally elided in verse for reasons I hope to make the subject of a special article (cf. Axelson, *Unpoetische Wörter*, pp. 83–4; Platnauer, p. 78 *et sq.*). Not elided in vv. 26, 57, ?17.

(c) *Anaphora*

The author is fond of this device, but uses it on one occasion with what seems to be a redundant conjunction—v. 77, . . . *nunc . . . et nunc*. . . . Birt, pp. 16–17, claims that such a use of the conjunction is at variance with that of the poets, but he admits a case of *modo . . . et modo*, F 1.129.

L. Otto[2] distinguishes (p. 71) five cases where the conjunction *et* may be found in *anaphora bipertita*, and the fifth case is where the introductory word is a *particle*. The example closest to our text is *iam . . . et iam* from *Aen.* 1.699. This, however, is not a case of *anaphora bipertita* (in view of Otto's statement (p. 68) 'Reliquum est ut doceamus hanc copulam [i.e. "et"] saepissime, et mira quadam licentia, abundantem ad singula anaphorae membra accedere. Quam etiam in anaphora bipertita solam admissam esse particulam . . . mirum est', it would seem that Vollmer's suggested *at* will not improve matters). The examples given by the *ThLL*, 5(2).899.41, are not very satisfactory: *Aen.* 10.805, Prop. 2.10.2, and Prop. 2.20.15 are hardly to be considered as parallel sentences. Even *Eleg. in Maecen.* 1.97, *tempora dispensant usus et tempora cultus* seems to need a conjunction. The real defence for the construction is rather to be sought in the fact that the *nunc* in the first clause (v. 77) is not the first word, and thus lacks the element of emphasis essential to anaphora. In any case *nunc* is not so strong a word as a noun or verb would be, although it is rather more emphatic than *iam*.

Ovid, it seems, would have used anaphora in vv. 2–6. Here there

[1] Ovid:

M	32
A, AA, RA, MF, Ep.	—
F, EP, T, Ibis	10

[2] Ludovicus Otto, *De anaphora; in exemplum adhibita sunt carmina Vergilii et Ovidii* (Diss. Marburg, 1907).

are a number of examples introduced with *sic* to illustrate the general truth which was enunciated in vv. 1–2. As Birt points out (p. 15), the practice of the poets is to introduce such lists with *sic* prefixed before each item and no conjunctions whatever, except when *sic et* is occasionally admitted. I have not been able to discover any case of *et sic* in such a list (*et sic* was not the subject of objection *per se*, cf. Lucr. 5.600, *quia sic . . . et sic . . .*; the anaphora is the real reason).

In our text the *sic* seems to lose all its retrospective force, for the clauses are joined with *et* or *que*, and the *sic* strays to fourth place in v. 6, and third place in v. 5; while even in the first clause it has second place. The lack of a particle in v. 4 is analogous to the cases where a conjunction is omitted. Something of the tendencies to be seen in vv. 2–6 may be noted in a long passage from Manilius (2.82 *et sq.*), *. . . deus et ratio . . . cogit . . . sentiri . . . ut . . . fata ministrent [signa] gentibus . . . nec nimis est quaerenda fides: sic temperat arua caelum, sic . . ., sic . . ., sic . . ., tu quoque fraternis* sic *reddis curribus ora, . . .*, denique sic *pecudes . . . sidera seruant . . .* (the proofs here are rather analogies than examples, but I do not see that this materially reduces the force of the parallel). Cf. also: *sic et . . . sic . . . sic et . . . ut, M* 5.815–16.

(d) *Irregular responsion*

The *ThLL*, 5(2).877.24, takes v. 9, *sic et scarus* as being a case of anacoluthon analogous ('forte') to *F* 6.224, *utilis et nuptis, utilis esse uiris*, etc. This seems to be unnecessary here, for the *sic et* may be taken as adding another example to the list which has preceded in vv. 2–6 (cf. *M* 15.855 *et sq.*; Manil. 4.815–16, etc.).

VV. 44–5: MORSU NEC COMMINUS ACRI DEFICIT, AUT ANIMOS PONIT CAPTIUA MINACIS. *neque . . . aut* is not too uncommon: *M* 9.614, *nec rigidas silices . . . solidumue in corpore ferrum, aut adamanta gerit, nec . . .*; Prop. 2.28.57, *nec forma aeternum, aut cuiquam est fortuna perennis.*

The *ThLL*, 2.1568.1, distinguishes cases where the *neque* is retrospective (i.e. *et non*) from those above. I cannot see that the examples quoted are convincing, but if, as I suspect, there is a gap in the text, we cannot really decide to which class this example belonged.

vv. 68–71: SEU . . . -UE CUM. . . . There seems to be no doubt but that these words have to be taken as correlative. If they are, then the information in Stolz-Schmalz (p. 676) about 'die Vermischung von *uel aut ue* (in nachklass. Zeit, seit Vitr., auch von *siue*)' and the consequences of their confusion (Vitr. 5.6.8, *aut . . . seu*) seems to indicate that this usage is careless but not alien to the period of Ovid (cf. Colum. 7.9.4, *uel cum . . . aut cum*). This is a poetic use which spread to the 'poetic' prose writers, and to writers in the vulgar language.

(e) *Subordinate conjunctions*

The use of *ut* to introduce examples[1] is seen in vv. 64–5 where it explains '*altera pars*', and it recurs in v. 118, *at contra herbosa pisces luxantur harena ut scarus.* . . . Normally there is some word in the principal sentence which carries the implication of a class as in Cic. *Tusc.* 4.25, ceteri *morbi, ut gloriae cupiditas, ut mulierositas*; Livy 2.48.6, alia *bella . . . instabant, ut ab Aequis Volscisque.* Examples may, however, be found of the use without a 'class-word', as in v. 118: Varro *Men.* 17, *terra culturae causa attributa olim hominibus, ut Etruria Tuscis, Samnium Sabellis*; *ibid.* 398, *poesis est perpetuum argumentum ex rhythmis, ut Ilias Homeri, et Annales Enni*; Hor. *sat.* 1.6.6, *ignotos, ut me libertino patre natum* (but the reading is doubtful here, cf. Palmer *ad loc.*); Hor. *sat.* 1.7.16, *si disparibus bellum incidat, ut Diomedi cum Lycio Glauco*; Quint. *inst.* 9.3.57, *inuenitur apud poetas, ut apud Homerum.* . . . This use seems fundamentally to be elliptic, and analogous to the use of *quales* in v. 94, which might be explained as: *nam gaudent pelago* [*tales pisces*] *quales* [*sunt*]. . . . I have not been able to find a satisfactory parallel. The omission of *tales* is not so difficult, but we have to understand the noun which is subject to *gaudent*, and the omission of *sunt* is awkward. Consequently we must doubt whether we have an astonishingly free use of *quales* or whether the text is corrupt.

(For the omission of *tales*, cf. Cic. *fam.* 6.6.8, *ingeniis excellentibus, quale est tuum, delectatur* (cf. Cic. *Lael.* 69) and a comparable omission of τοῖος in Greek—e.g. Aeschylus, *Persae* 882.)

(f) *Postponement of conjunctions*

(i) *Co-ordinate*

MORSU NEC (v. 44); PRESSUS ET (v. 62). Haupt (*Opuscula* i.123) has shown that Ovid practically never postpones *et* in the Metamorphoses although he does so quite freely in the elegiac poems (he allows *M* 15.444 as a special case; Artymowicz, *WSt* 31 (1909), p. 39, cites *M* 1.638; *M* 8.247; *M* 10.207—I take the last example

---

[1] Cf. Bastian Dahl, *Die lateinische Partikel UT*, Kristiania, 1882, whence my examples are taken ('*Ut exempli*', p. 111). The use in our text would seem, from the examples in Varro and Hor. *sat.*, to be conversational.

as *etiam*; cf. Platnauer, pp. 94–5). I have seen no reference to a postponement of *nec* in the Metamorphoses; Platnauer (*loc. cit.*) states that only two cases (*Ep.* 16.346; *EP* 3.3.42) occur in the hexameters of the elegiac poems, and ten in the pentameters (Maecenas had no inhibitions on this score: *lucentes mea uita nec smaragdos . . .*, etc., *fr.* 1). In our text, however, there may well be a notion of *ne comminus quidem* (cf. Ehwald on *M* 11.471) that attracts the *nec* to its place in the sentence.

I reject *prodigus atque* (v. 57) and *auersus crebro uimen sed* (v. 13) as improbable conjectures for other reasons.[1] The former is not to be paralleled from Ovid[2] (*atque*, *AA* 3.282 is rightly questioned by Haupt, *Opusc.* i.125); Lygdamus 5.28 is the only case of postponement of *sed* to the fourth place that I have been able to trace (cf. Platnauer, *loc. cit.*).

(ii) *enclitic*

UIM SPINAE NOUITQUE SUAE (v. 47); INSIGNIS SARGUSQUE NOTIS (v. 105). The only case I have found in the *Metamorphoses* is *poteras certeque* (14.30; cf. Housman, *CQ* 10 (1916), p. 149). Vergil has examples in *Geo.* 3.238; 2.95; I am very doubtful about *Aen.* 6.254; 818 cited by Leo (p. 429). Norden, p. 404, adn. (4), describes *Geo.* 2.95; 3.238 and *Aen.* 6.818 as 'drei sichere Beispiele'. Leo remarks the cases in the *Halieutica* as strange,[3] but adds the saver 'wenn ich nicht irre'. However, Norden (*loc. cit.*) remarks that Horace in his *Satires* uses the postponement frequently, and it is a well-known feature of the pentameter in the elegiac poets. Leo also remarks on the frequent occurrence in later metrical inscriptions.

---

[1] Cf. Commentary.   [2] But cf. Levy on *T* 3.2.13.
[3] Even in elegiacs, 'Postponed enclitics are found much more rarely in the hexameter: of this there are two cases in Tib. I and II, two or three in Propertius, and perhaps six in Ovid' (Platnauer, p. 92).

Prepositions

Ab

UIRIDENTUR AB HERBIS (v. 90): on considering *A* 2.5.39, *longis flauescere . . . ab annis*, and *F* 5.323, *caelum nigrescit ab austris*, it is rather tempting to imagine that the verb may not be passive here. Still, the invariable use of the active forms, and the parallel quoted from Valerius[1] both weigh against any such view.

Ad

AD LAXATA . . . CONIXA FORAMINA RETIS (v. 28): is this 'striving toward the loosened meshes' or 'straining against the loosened meshes'? The parallel passages seem to favour the former version, for they both mention the *murenae* seeking the loosened mesh, and then wriggling through. Usage, too, seems to favour this interpretation, for Vergil (*Aen.* 11.612) uses the word of a charge with lances: *continuo aduersis . . . conixi incurrunt hastis*; Val. Max. 2.7.2 (*ad reuocandam . . . disciplinam . . . conisus est*) suggests *opus aggredi*; cf. Cic. *Cato* (82) . . . *animus maxime ad immortalitatem . . . niteretur*, Tac. *Ann.* 15.66.2. On the other hand, 'to strain, or lean against' is improbable, for to get a usage of even *niti ad* in the sense of 'lean on' seems difficult. The example given by the *ThLL* (1.475.58), Prop. 3.3.14, *sic ait aurata nixus ad antra lyra*, may be defended by Prop. 4.1.110, *haerentis ad pia saxa rates*; but if *nixus* goes with *ad antra*, then we must take *ait* with *aurata lyra*—which seems odd. I prefer 'near the caves, resting on his golden lyre'. So Postgate: '*lyra nixus*. Apollo is frequently thus represented in art.'

Per

The use of *per* in DEDIT . . . PER OMNES (v. 1) is normal if *dare* can mean *distribuere*; cf. Commentary.

PER MULTOS EUADIT . . . FLEXUS (v. 29): cf. Commentary. The construction was, perhaps, felt as local, but the force is rather modal, the idea being as in Verg. *Geo.* 1.244, *flexu sinuoso elabitur Anguis*.

INMITIS . . . PER UULNERA (v. 115): this seems to mean 'cruel by means of his wounds'. It may be paralleled by *Ep.* 12.41, *Martis erant*

[1] On v. 90, *sup.*

tauri plus quam per cornua saeui, and *Ibis* 358, *per crimen sit tibi fida soror*, but these instrumental uses depending on adjectives are the only two cases I have traced in Ovid that are entirely satisfactory (cf. discussion in my commentary). However, the example of *per* with the agent in *M* 7.40, *per me sospes*, shows how the *constructio ad sensum* (*M* 7.40 just means *per me conseruatus*) inevitably extended the use dependent on participles to that in the text. Our example is curiously reminiscent of *F* 5.468, *mitior illa fuit*; *crudelem animam per uulnera reddas*, where our author may have taken *crudelem* with *per uulnera*. We cannot take *per* as meaning *propter*, for it does not give clear sense. This usage is non-classical, save for certain set phrases (Stolz-Schmalz, p. 438). Cf. Riemann, p. 184, who quotes from Quintilian; there are many examples in the *Lexicon Taciteum*, pp. 1096–7. See also Bährens, *Glotta* 4 (1913), p. 278, who quotes Frontinus 2.3.17; p. 51.4.

Sub

SUB LEGE LOCI (v. 33): Birt (p. 76) attacks this phrase on the ground that *sub* was used only in certain set phrases like *sub lege ne*, *sub condicione ut*, etc. This seems a little too rigid for poetry, cf. *accipe sub certa condicione preces*, *F* 4.320. The presence of a redundant *sub* in *nullo sub teste*, Juv. 15.26, is characterized by Duff as 'idiomatic . . . *nullo teste* would mean the same, cf. 10.70'. I should prefer to imagine that the analogy of common phrases has been pressed into service to satisfy the necessity of the metre.

UIMEN SUB UERBERE CAUDAE LAXANS SUBSEQUITUR (vv. 13–14): Pliny, who paraphrases (32.11) with *caudae ictibus crebris laxare fores*, seems to have read *sub* as being instrumental. Kühner 2.1.571, remarks 'Im spätl. findet sich dann auch der Übergang in die instrumentale Bedeutung',[1] so we can hardly allow an instrumental usage here. The opening nominative *auersus* strongly inclines the reader to make *laxans*, although a second participle, agree with it. It then becomes hard to explain the necessity for *sub* and the meaning of *laxans subsequitur*.

I believe that, as in other cases, the clue to the true interpretation here is to be sought from the passage imitated by the author. Vergil's *torto uolitans sub uerbere turbo* (*Aen.* 7.378) indicates that in our text we should join *uimen* and *laxans* and translate 'he follows closely

---

[1] 'der Übergang', that is, from the *sub* of attendant circumstances in such phrases as Prop. 2.28.35, *magico torti sub carmine rhombi*. Cf. also Palmer on *Ep.* 13.71, *cadere* . . . *sub milite Troiam*: ' "beneath" from the idea of a form prostrate under the victor; the idea of agency does not belong to *sub* as to ὑπό'. Ehwald on *M* 5.62, *exhalantem sub acerbo uulnere uitam*, takes *sub* as 'causal'. He quotes no parallels.

the wicker work which loosens under the lash of his tail' (cf. also *citus . . . uerbere turben*, Tib. 1.5.3). This implies that *laxare* is used intransitively. That *laxare* may have been used intransitively cannot be denied (cf. Livy 26.20.11, *annona haud multum laxauerat*), but the only example that I have been able to trace, which is like the use I assume in our text, is Curtius 4.3.6, *crebris fluctibus compages operis uerberatae laxauere*. It is most remarkable that here the vocabulary (*crebris*—cf. *crebro*, v. 13; *uerberatae*—cf. *uerbere*, v. 13) suggests some connexion with our passage. From Tac. *Ann.* 6.24.3, . . . *ut . . . ostenderet nepotem sub uerbere centurionis, inter seruorum ictus extrema uitae alimenta frustra orantem*, it seems that *sub uerbere* just meant 'under the lash'. I think that is a strong argument in favour of my interpretation.

I admit, of course, that here again, as in *sub lege loci*, v. 33, analogy may have influenced the author to give a quasi-instrumental force to *sub*; cf. Manil. 3.42, *propria melius sub uoce notantur*.

Lack of prepositions

?TERGO (v. 46), IMO (v. 90): cf. Stolz-Schmalz, p. 451, 'freier verfahren die Dichter (vgl. Cic. *fin.* 5.9, *ut nulla pars, caelo mari terra, ut poetice loquar, praetermissa sit*). So Catull. Hor. Prop. Tib. (1.5.53, *herbasque sepulcris quaerat*)'. I have not seen it remarked in Ovid. (It is just possible that the author felt that *subnatis* governed *imo*, but one would expect that then the meaning would be 'having grown under the sea-bed' rather than 'having grown below on the sea-bed'.)

(UULNERE . . . LAXATO CADAT HAMUS (v. 41), is the regular construction with the verb. Perhaps the ablatives are in the absolute construction; cf. *M* 11.516 for a similar ambiguity.)

Abundance of prepositions

A number of the cases above come under this heading, for the simple ablative would alone suffice. This is a common feature of poetic style,[1] and represents the tendency in the spoken language.

[1] Cf. *Lucretius*, ed. Bailey, i, 106 (ed. 1947).

Note on the order of the items in the catalogue (vv.94-134) and in Pliny 32.152-3

Fish	verse in Hal.	Order in Plin. 32.152		Order in Plin. 32.153	
boues	94	bouem	(a)		
helops	96			helopem	(5)†
pompil*us*	101			pompilum	(3)
cercyros	102	cercyrum	(b)		
orphus	104	orphum	(c)		
erythinus	104	erythinum	(d)		
iulis	105	iulum	(e)		
channe	108			channen	(1)
mormyres	110	mormyras	(f)		
chrysophrys	111	chrysophryn	(g)		
percae	112	?percam	(h)		
tragi	112	tragum	(i)		
melanurus	113	melanurum	(j)		
glaucus	117			glaucum	(2)
chromis	121			chromin	(4)
lepores	126	lepores	(k)		
acipenser	134			acipenserem	(5)†

From this table it will be clear that Pliny indicates that the *iulis* must occur in the catalogue between the *erythinus* (v. 104), and the *mormyres* (v. 110).

It will also be noted that in 32.153 the order does seem in some degree to have been preserved, but, as explained in notes on v. 101, and in *Ovidiana*, p. 454 *et sq.*, it does not seem to be possible to restore it almost completely by transferring the *pompilus* to a place after the *glaucus* in v. 117. It seems evident that the *helops* was suggested by the *acipenser*, when Pliny came to the place of the latter.

APPENDIX 4

Greek terminations

I set out a list of the words which show Greek terminations.

(a) *Forms guaranteed by the metre*

xiphias	v. 97
synodontĕs	v. 107
channe	v. 108
mormyrĕs	v. 110

(b) *Forms not guaranteed by the metre*

anthias	v. 46	(?—metrical difficulty)
cercyros	v. 102	
chrysophrys	v. 111	
scorpios	v. 116	(?—Ms. scorpio)
lamiros	v. 120	

APPENDIX 5

Imitations in the *Halieutica*

For the convenience of readers I set out tables[1] showing the imitations and reminiscences which I believe I have traced in the *Halieutica*. Lenz sets out in his edition the chief passages that are parallel to the accounts in our poem of the fishes' wiles. The following additions to Lenz's passages may be found useful:

Hal.

9–18   Cassiodorus *uar.* 11.40.8.

23–26   Cassiodorus *uar.* 11.40.7.

43–45   Philo Iudaeus *Alexander, seu de animalibus* 36 (cf. notes on v. 44).

---

[1] They have already been printed in *Atti*, p. 42 *et sq.*, but the proofs of that article were never submitted to me, with the result that the tables there are disarranged.

Major imitations

Hal. 1 *et sq.*,

. . . .
accepit mundus legem. dedit arma per omnes,
admonuitque sui. uitulus sic †manuque† minatur
qui nondum gerit in tenera iam cornua fronte,
sic dammae fugiunt, pugnant uirtute leones,
et morsu canis, et caudae sic scorpius ictu,
concussisque leuis pinnis sic euolat ales.

Hal. 53 *et sq.*,
inpiger ecce leo uenantum sternere pergit
agmina et aduersis infert sua pectora telis!
quoque uenit fidens magis et sublatior ardet
(concussitque toros, et uiribus addidit iram),
. . . .
†prodedit† atque suo properat sibi robore letum.

Hal. 58 *et sq.*,
foedus Lucanis prouoluitur ursus ab antris:
quid nisi pondus iners, stolidique...

Hal. 60 *et sq.*,

. . . .
actus aper saetis iram denuntiat hirtis,
se ruit oppositi nitens in uulnera ferri,
pressus et emisso moritur per uiscera telo.

lingua suas *accepit* barbara *leges*.   Manil. 1.85.

denique sic pecudes, et muta animalia terris,
cum maneant *ignara sui*, legisque per aeuum,
natura tamen ad *mundum* reuocante parentem,
adtollunt animos...etc.   Manil. 2.99 *et sq.*

cornua nata prius uitulo quam frontibus extent,
illis iratus petit, atque infestus inurget;
at catuli pantherarum, scymnique leonum,
unguibus ac pedibus iam tum morsuque repugnant
uix etiam cum sunt dentes unguesque creati;
alituum porro genus alis omne uidemus
fidere, et a pinnis tremulum petere auxiliatum.
                                        Lucr. 5.1034 *et sq.*

.................qualis...........
saucius ille graui *uenantum* uulnere *pectus*
tum demum mouet arma leo, gaudetque comantis
excutiens ceruice *toros*, fixumque latronis
impauidus frangit telum, et fremit ore cruento.
                                        Aen. 12.4 *et sq.*

...................sicut squalentibus aruis
aestiferae Libyes uiso leo comminus hoste,
subsedit dubius totam dum *colligit iram*,
mox ubi se saeuae stimulauit uerbere caudae,
erexitque iubam, et uasto graue murmur hiatu
infremuit, tum torta leuis si lancea Mauri
haereat, aut latum subeant uenabula *pectus*,
per ferrum tanti securus uolneris exit.
                                        Lucan. 1.205 *et sq.*

Pannonis haud aliter post ictum saeuior ursa,
cum iaculum parua Libys ammentauit habena,
se rotat in uulnus, telumque irata receptum
impetit, et secum fugientem circumit hastam.
                                        Lucan. 6.220 *et sq.*

ac uelut ille canum morsu de montibus altis
actus aper......postquam inter retia uentum est,
substitit, infremuitque ferox...
                                        Aen. 10.707 *et sq.*

Hal. 66 *et sq.,*
　　hic generosus honos et gloria maior equorum:
　　nam cupiunt animis palmam gaudentque triumpho,
　　seu septem spatiis circo meruere coronam
　　(nonne uides uictor quanto sublimius altum
　　adtollat caput, et uulgi se uenditet aurae?)
　　celsaue cum caeso decorantur terga leone
　　(quam tumidus, quantoque uenit spectabilis actu,
　　conspissatque solum generoso concita pulsu
　　ungula sub spoliis grauiter redeuntis opimis!)

Hal. 75 *et sq.,*
　　quin laus prima canum, quibus est audacia praeceps,
　　uenandique sagax uirtus, uiresque sequendi.
　　quae nunc elatis rimantur naribus auram,
　　et nunc demisso quaerunt uestigia rostro,
　　et produnt clamore feram (dominumque uocando
　　increpitant), quam, si conlatis effugit armis,
　　insequitur tumulosque canis camposque per omnis.

Hal. 103,
　　cantharus ingratus suco...

Hal. 119,
　　...scarus, epastas solus qui ruminat escas.

primam merui...coronam...
>
> *Aen.* 5.355.

..........................cauatque
tellurem, et solido grauiter sonat ungula cornu.
>
> *georg.* 3.87 *et sq.*

nunc dimissi nare sagaci
captant auras, lustraque presso
quaerunt rostro.
>
> Seneca, *Phaedra* 40 *et sq.*

sic cum feras uestigat, et longo sagax
loro tenetur Vmber, ac presso uias
scrutatur ore, dum procul lento suem
odore sentit, paret, et tacito locum
rostro pererrat; praeda cum propior fuit
ceruice tota pugnat, et gemitu uocat
dominum morantem, seque retinenti eripit.
>
> Seneca *Thy.* 497 *et sq.*

cantharidum sucos, dante parente, bibas.
>
> Ov. *Ibis* 308.

...lente reuocatas ruminat herbas
atque iterum pasto pascitur ante cibo.
>
> (?Ov.) *Am.* 3.5.17.

hic uomit epotas dira Charybdis aquas.
>
> Ov. *Rem.* 740.

Minor imitations and parallels

Halieutica		Ovid
3. gerit in tenera iam cornua fronte	cornua fronte gerit	*Met.* 15.596 *et al.*
6. euolat ales	euolat alis	*Met.* 1.264
18. seruato . . . ciue	seruatos ciuis	*Trist.* 3.1.48
20. manus timet illa rapacis	urentes effugit illa manus	*Fast.* 4.706
21. uomit illa cruorem	uomit ille cruorem	*Met.* 5.83
26. dolos saltu deludit inultus	et mecum lusos ridet inulta deos	*Am.* 3.3.20
27. teretis sibi conscia tergi	diri sibi conscia facti	*Met.* 8.531
33. sub lege loci	lege loci	*Ars.* 1.142
35. hic quoque fallit	sic quoque fallebant	*Met.* 1.698
38. euerberat escam	euerberat alis	*Met.* 14.577
43. uires . . . nocendi	uires . . . nocendi	*Met.* 7.417
45. animos . . . minacis	animosque minacis	*Met.* 6.688
49. cetera quae densas habitant animalia siluas	cetera . . . animalia densis . . . siluis	*Met.* 1.416
		Met. 15.488
56. addidit iram	addidit iram	*Met.* 12.532 *et al.*
59. quid nisi pondus iners	nec quicquam nisi pondus iners	*Met.* 1.6
61. ruit . . . nitens in uulnera ferri	in ferrum flammasque ruit	*Ars.* 2.379
65. sine fine	sine fine	*Trist.* 2.63 *et al.*
66. honos et gloria maior	maior honos coniunctaque gloria	*Met.* 13.96
69. nonne uides?	nonne uides?	*Met.* 5.375
78. et nunc demisso quaerunt uestigia rostro	extento stringit uestigia rostro	*Met.* 1.536
86–7. talia lentos deposcunt calamos	talia deposcunt	*Met.* 1.200
89. fugiuntque petuntque	fugiuntque petuntque	*Ars.* 1.545
117. aestiuo . . . sidere	brumali sidere	*Pont.* 2.4.25

13. uerbere caudae	uerbera caudae	Hor. *sat.* 2.7.49
	uerbere caudae	Lucan. 1.208
18. quem téxit	quae téxit	Manil. 1.781
19. tarda fugae	tardusque fugae	Val. Flacc. 3.547
25. in auras emicat	per auras emicat	Homer. 86
51. trahit in praeceps	in praeceps...rapit	(trahit *Codex R*)
		georg. 1.203
54. aduersis infert sua pectora telis	aduersum fidens fer pectus in hostem	*Aen.* 11.370
57. properat sibi robore letum	properet per uulnera mortem	*Aen.* 9.401
68. circo meruere coronam	primam merui... coronam	*Aen.* 5.355
71. caeso...leone	caeso...iuuenco	Lucan. 4.132
75. quin laus prima canum...	prima illa canum [cura]	Gratt. 151
audacia praeceps	audacia praeceps	Claudian 3.34
76. uenandique sagax uirtus uiresque sequendi	inuictus canis nare sagax et uiribus fretus	Enn. *Ann.* 533 (Vah.) (*coni.*)
77. quae nunc elatis rimantur naribus auram	lucemque elatis naribus efflant	*Aen.* 12.115 (cf. Enn. *Ann.* 588 (Vah.))
81. tumulosque... camposque per omnis	fertur in arua furens cumulo, camposque per omnis	*Aen.* 2.498
	circum collis, camposque per omnis	Lucr. 5.784
88. horrentes...umbras	horrenti...umbra	*Aen.* 1.165
122. dulces nidos	dulces...nidi	*Aen.* 5.214
	dulcis...nidos	*georg.* 1.414

8*

APPENDIX 6

Prosodical Difficulties

Greek words

ANTHIAS, v. 46: the final vowel is long by nature. If the Ms. reading is to stand, we must either postulate a completely arbitrary shortening of the final syllable, or claim that the last two vowels have suffered a synizesis for which no parallel can be found in a Greek word in the Roman poets of the first century A.D.

POMPILE, v. 101: the penultimate vowel is short by nature, but it must be taken as long to scan in our verse.

MORMYRES, v. 110: this form is not found in Greek, but analogy with μορμύρος and μορμύλος would indicate that the penultimate is short. In our text it must be taken as long.

CHRYSOPHRYS, v. 111: this word has a short final syllable in Greek, but the long syllable in our text is presumably the result of the not unusual lengthening before the strong caesura. Alternatively, it may be due to analogy with the word ὀφρῦς of which it is a compound.

LAMIROS, v. 120: Birt, p. 116, relies on the very doubtful analogies of λάρινος and λάριμος, and asserts that the first syllable of this word should properly be long. He thinks that the shortening here is due to the licence frequently taken by the poets in dealing with proper names.

Latin words

EI, v. 34: see my commentary for discussion.

MILUI, v. 95: this word has three syllables in the following passages: *A* 2.6.34, *M* 2.716, *F* 3.794,809, Phaedrus 1.31.3,10, Persius 4.26, Mart. 9.54.10. In our text it is disyllabic. The earliest other example of the disyllabic pronunciation is to be found in Juv. 9.55. Maurenbrecher, p. 208, claims that the vowel *u*, when preceded by a long vowel and a liquid, and followed by a vowel (e.g. *larua* and *peluis*), began to change to the consonantal pronunciation in the time of Horace. His examples are few, and mostly not very convincing.

Birt, p. 116 *et sq.*, had defended the lengthenings in *pompile* and *mormyres* as being due to the Greek accent. Housman (*CQ* 1 (1907), p. 275 *et sq.*) pointed out that the metrical anomalies in our poem

are completely unparalleled in the Latin poets of the first century
A.D., and asks how we can believe that our poem was ever read by
Pliny the Elder. Lenz, p. 17 *et sq.*, tries to defend the usages as
Ovidian! He says that *anthias* could not have been made to scan
(yet Ovid would surely have used *anthia*, cf. *Aeeta*, M 7.170, *Marsya*,
M 6.400, and Housman, *JPh* 31 (1910), p. 241), and that hence the
poet had no option but to ignore the proper scansion. He thinks the
passage from Juvenal sufficient defence for *miluus*. He admits that
pompile is a solecism, but not one great enough to subvert the attribu-
tion by Pliny. Lenz does not find it necessary to adopt the suggestion
made by Owen (*CQ* 8 (1914), p. 271 *et sq.*) that Ovid's pronunciation
had been corrupted by the fishermen of Tomi, and his use of the Getic
language. Owen (ibid., p. 27 *et sq.*) had already tried to defend such
variations in quantity, and Lenz refers the reader to some irrelevant
material collected by K. P. Schulze in *BPhW* 39 (1919), col. 283
et sq.

ADDITIONAL NOTES

p. 25 (TITLE): for Pliny's use of the genitive in *nat.* 32.11, *quod Halieuticon inscribitur*, cf. *AA* 3.343, *titulo quos signat Amorum*, and E. Löfstedt, *Late Latin* (Oslo, 1959), p. 134.

p. 44 (**36**): Manil. 1.116, *ut possim rerum tantas emergere moles*, is a much more satisfactory example of transitive *emergere*. The reflexive use with *se* is quite common, of course.

p. 59 (**65a**) SEQUI NATURA MONET: cf. Plin. *nat.* 18.227, [*natura*] *monet festinare*.

p. 65 (**75**) LAUS PRIMA CANUM: the following passages should also be noted—Verg. *Geo.* 3.404, *nec tibi cura canum fuerit postrema*; Nemesianus *cyneg.* 103, *principio tibi cura canum . . . ab anno incipiat primo*; Orosius *hist.* 1 prol. 3, *non est tamen canum cura postrema; quibus solis natura insitum est uoluntarie ad id quod praeparabantur urgueri. . . .* They seem to favour the view of O. Skutsch that *prima* in our text is predicative.

p. 83 (**115**) CANCER PER UULNERA: O. Skutsch suggests that this may be the ghost of an etymology, and compares Apul. *apol.* 35, *qui minus possit . . . calculus ad uesicam, testa ad †testamentum†, cancer ad ulcera, alga ad quercerum.*

p. 100: the redundant use of *sub* is noted by Housman on Manil. 1.845, and was also discussed by him in a paper read to the Cambridge Philological Society, an abstract of which was published in the *Cambridge University Reporter* of 8 Nov. 1927.

INDEX BIBLIOGRAPHICVS

The Bibliography which follows includes all works known to me which I believe to be of importance for the study of the *Halieutica*, and some other books which are of use in considering the kind of problem which one meets in reading such a text. A useful list of concordances of the Latin poets will be found on p. 11 of B. Axelson's *Unpoetische Wörter*.

ANDRÉ, J., *Étude sur les termes de couleur dans la langue latine*, Paris, 1949

AXELSON, B., 'Eine Ovidische Echtheitsfrage' in *Eranos* 43 (1945), p. 23 *et sq.* (cf. 39 (1941), p. 74)
Unpoetische Wörter ... (Skrifter utgiv. av Vetenskaps-soc. i Lund, 29), Lund, 1945

BAEHRENS, E., Review in *Jenaer Literaturzeitung* 6 (1879), p. 252 *et sq.*

BÄHRENS, W. A., *Sprachlicher Kommentar zur* ... *Appendix Probi*, Halle, 1922

BARTH, C. VON (Caspar Barthius), *Adversariorum commentariorum libri LX* [see lib. XLIX cap. 7], Frankfurt, 1624

BEDNARA, E., 'De sermone dactylicorum ... (II)' in *ALL* 14 (1906), p. 532 *et sq.*

BIRT, T., *De Halieuticis Ovidio poetae falso adscriptis*, Berlin, 1878
Kritik und Hermeneutik [see p. 231], Munich, 1913
Das antike Buchwesen [see p. 298, footnote], Berlin, 1882

BOISACQ, É., *Dictionnaire étymologique de la langue grecque*, ed. 4, Heidelberg, 1950

BONAPARTE (PRINCE CHARLES), *Iconografia della fauna Italica*, 3 tom., Rome, 1832–41

BRENOUS, J., *Étude sur les hellénismes dans la syntaxe latine*, Paris, 1895

BRUNN, H. VON, *De auctorum indicibus Plinianis disputatio isagogica*, Bonn, 1856

BÜCHELER, F., *Kleine Schriften*, Band 3 [p. 230] (or *RhM* 51 (1896), p. 326), Leipzig, 1930

CHATELAIN, E., *Paléographie des classiques latins*, Paris, 1884–92

CLARK, A. C., *The Descent of Manuscripts*, Oxford, 1918

CLIFT, E. H., *Latin Pseudepigrapha* [practically useless; see p. 134], Baltimore, 1945

COTTE, H. J., *Poissons et animaux aquatiques au temps de Pline* ... (Diss., Paris), Aix, 1944

CURCIO, G., *see*: OVIDIUS NASO, P., *Halieutica*

DRAEGER, A., *Ovid als Sprachbildner* (Prog.), Aurich, 1888
Ueber Syntax und Stil des Tacitus, 3te Aufl., Leipzig, 1882

EINLEITUNG IN DIE ALTERTUMSWISSENSCHAFT, *see*: GERCKE, A., and NORDEN, E.

ENCICLOPEDIA ITALIANA, Rome, 1929–39

ENNIUS, Q., *Quae supersunt fragmenta*, ed. H. Columna, Naples, 1590

ERDMANN, O., *Über den Gebrauch der lateinischen Adjektiva mit Genetiv* ... (Prog.), Stendal, 1879

FOHALLE, R., 'Sur la vocabulaire maritime...' in *Mélanges ... Paul Thomas* [p. 271 *et sq.*], Bruges, 1930

FRÄNKEL, H., *Ovid: a poet between two worlds*, Berkeley (Cal.), 1945

GANZENMÜLLER, C., 'Aus Ovids Werkstatt' in *Ph* 70 (1911), p. 274 *et sq.*; p. 397 *et sq.*

GERBER, A., and GREEF, A., *Lexicon Taciteum*, Leipzig, 1895–1903

GERCKE, A., and NORDEN, E., *Einleitung in die Altertumswissenschaft*, vol. 1, 1ste Aufl., Leipzig, 1910; 3te Aufl., Leipzig, 1923

GRATTIUS, *Cynegeticon* ... ed. P. J. Enk, 2 vols., Zutphen, 1918
see also: R. STERN

HACKMANN, F., *De Athenaeo Naucratita quaestiones selectae* (Diss.), Berlin, 1912

HARTEL, W., Review in *ZöG* 17 (1866), p. 334 *et sq.*

HAVET, (P. A.) L., *Manuel de critique verbale* . . ., Paris, 1911

HAUPT, M., see also: OVIDIUS NASO, P., *Halieutica*
    Opuscula, vol. 1, Leipzig, 1875

HAUSTEIN, A., *De genetivi adiectivis accomodati in lingua latina usu* (Diss.), Halle, 1882

HILBERG, I., *Die Gesetze der Wortstellung im Pentameter des Ovid*, Leipzig, 1894

HIPPOCRATES, *Hippocratis et aliorum medicorum veterum reliquiae*, ed. F. Z. Ermerins, 3 vols. [contains the ps-Hippocratic *De uictus ratione*], Utrecht, 1859–64

HOUSMAN, A. E., 'Versus Ouidi de piscibus et feris' in *CQ* 1 (1907), p. 275 *et sq.*

JACOBI, O. E., *De syntaxi in Ovidii Tristibus et Epistulis ex Ponto observata* (Diss.), Lyck (East Prussia), 1870

JONES, L. W., *The script of Cologne*, Cambridge (Mass.), 1932

JORDAN, D. S., *A guide to the study of fishes*, 2 vols., Westminster (U.S.A.), 1905

IUVENALIS, DECIMUS IUNIUS, *Index verborum Iuvenalis*, by L. Kelling and A. Suskin, Chapel Hill (N. Car.), 1951

KELLER, O., *Zur lateinischen Sprachgeschichte*, 2 Bände: Band 2: *Grammatische Aufsätze*, Leipzig, 1895
    Die antike Tierwelt, 2 Bände: Band 2, Leipzig, 1913

KEYDELL, R., 'Oppians Gedicht von der Fischerei und Aelians Tier-geschichte' in *Hermes* 72 (1937), p. 411 *et sq.*

KIENZLE, L., *Die Kopulativpartikeln et, -que, atque bei Tacitus, Plinius, Seneca*, Tübingen, 1906

KÜHNER, R., *Ausführliche Grammatik der lateinischen Sprache*, 2 Bände, Hanover, 1912–14

LACHMANN, K., *Kleinere Schriften*, Band 2, Berlin, 1876

LENZ, F. W. (formerly Levy, F. W.), see also: OVIDIUS NASO, P., *Halieutica* review in *Sokrates* 76 (1922), p. 143 *et sq.*

LEO, F., 'Bemerkungen über plautinische Wortstellung und Wortgruppen', in *Nachrichten von der königl. Gesellschaft der Wissenschaften zu Göttingen, philologisch-historische Klasse*, 1895, p. 415 *et sq.*

LEUMANN, M., *Die lateinischen Adjektiva auf* -lis . . . (Untersuch. z. idg. Sprach-und Kulturwiss., vii), Strassburg, 1917

LEYHAUSEN (C.) J., *Helenae et Herus epistolae Ovidii non sunt* (Diss.), Halle, 1893

LINDSAY, W. M., *An introduction to Latin textual emendation based on the text of Plautus*, London, 1896
    Notae Latinae, Cambridge, 1915

LINSE, E., *De P. Ovidio Nasone vocabulorum inventore* (Diss.), Tübingen, 1891

LODGE, G., *Lexicon Plautinum*, 2 vols., Leipzig, 1904–33

LOEW, E. A., see: LOWE, E. A.

LÖWE (E.), *Über die Präpositionen A, De, Ex bei Ovid.* (Prog.), Strehlen, 1889

LÖFSTEDT, (H.) E. (H.), *Beiträge zur Kenntnis der späteren Latinität* (Diss.), Uppsala, 1907
    Spätlateinische Studien (Skrifter . . . K. Hum. Vet.-sam., Uppsala, 12:4), Leipzig, 1908

Syntactica, erster Teil, 2te Aufl. (Skrifter utgiv. av K. Human. Veten-
skapssampf. i Lund. 10:1), Lund, 1942

LOWE, E. A., *The Beneventan Script*, Oxford, 1914
Codices Latini Antiquiores (in progress), Oxford, 1934—
Scriptura Beneventana, Oxford, 1929
'Studia palaeographica' (*Sitzungsber. d. koen. bay. Akad. d. Wiss., philos.-philol.-hist. Kl.*, 1910, *Abh.* 12)

LUCILIUS, C., *C. Lucili carminum reliquiae*, ed. F. Marx, 2 vols. [*see*: p. lii],
Leipzig, 1904–5

MAAS, P., 'Studien zum poetischen Plural . . .' in *ALL* 12 (1902), p. 477
et sq.

MALLON, J. AND ORS., *L'écriture latine de la capitale romaine à la minuscule*,
Paris, 1939

MARTIALIS, M. VALERIUS, *Epigrammaton libri*, ed. W. Heraeus, Leipzig, 1925

MARTINI, E., *Einleitung zu Ovid* [bibliography of the *Hal.*], Brünn, 1933

MAURENBRECHER, B., *Parerga zur lateinischen Sprachgeschichte und zum Thesaurus*,
Leipzig, 1916

MOREL, W. (ed.), *Fragmenta poetarum latinorum*, neue Ausg., Leipzig, 1927

MÜLLER, L., *De re metrica poetarum latinorum . . .*, ed. 2, Leipzig, 1894

MÜNZER, F., *Beiträge zur Quellenkritik der Naturgeschichte des Plinius*, Berlin,
1897

NEUE, F. and WAGENER, C., *Formenlehre der lateinischen Sprache,* 3te Aufl.,
4 Bände, Leipzig, 1892–1905

NORDEN, E., see: VERGILIUS MARO, P.

NORMAN, J. R., *A History of Fishes* (ed. 1), London, 1931

OPPIANUS, *Halieutica*
in *Oppian, Colluthus, Tryphiodorus*, ed. A. W. Mair, London, 1928

OTTO, L., *De anaphora: in exempla adhibita sunt carmina Vergilii et Ovidii* (Diss.),
Marburg, 1907

'OVIDIANA', *Ovidiana, recherches sur Ovide, publiées . . . par N. I. Herescu*, Paris,
1958

OVIDIUS NASO, P., *Halieutica*
Halieuticon liber acephalus . . . [with Grattius and Nemesianus], ed. G.
Logus,[1] Venice, 1534
P. Ovidii Halieuticon, ed. C. Gesner, Zürich, 1556
in *Venatus et aucupium iconibus artificiosis ad vivum expressa*, Frankfurt, 1582
in *P. Ovidii Nasonis epistolae heroides Hercule Ciofano Sulmonensi . . . emendatae*,
ed. 2 [p. 85 *et sq.*], Antwerp, 1582
in *Epigrammata et poematia vetera*, ed. P. Pithoeus [pp. 90–94, second
pagination], Paris, 1590
in *Operum quae extant tomus III . . . postrema Iacobi Micylli recognitione et
recensione nova Gregorii Bersmani . . .* editio tertia, Leipzig, 1596
in the *Venatio nov-antiqua* of J. Vlitius (J. van Vliet), (Leyden), 1645
in *Operum P. Ovidii Nasonis editio nova; Nic. Heinsius Dan. F. recensuit ac
notas addidit*, Amsterdam, 1661

[1] According to Curcio there is an edition by Vascosani, (Paris, 1542,) but I have
not been able to trace it.

in *Opera omnia cum integris Nicolai Heinsii notis studio B. Cnipingii*, Leyden, 1670

in *Heroides* . . . *Halieutica integris Iacobi Micylli, Herculis Ciofani, Danielis et Nicolai Heinsiorum, et excerptis aliorum notis, quibus suas adiecit Petrus Burmannus* (Tom. I of the *Opera omnia*), Amsterdam, 1727

in *I frammenti di P. Ovidio Nasone*, tr. P. Salandri, Milan, 1752 (cf. *Corpus omnium veterum poetarum latinorum*, vol. 30, Milan, 1754, and *Alcune opere di P. Ovidio Nasone*, Messina, 1754)

in *Poetae latini minores*, ed. J. C. Wernsdorf, 6 vols. [vol. 1, p. 141], Altenburg, 1780–99 (reprinted by Lemair with minor changes (in Bibl. Classica Latina, vol. 134), Paris, 1824)

in *Ovidii Halieutica* . . ., ed. M. Haupt, Leipzig, 1838

in *Opera*, vol. 3, ed. R. Merkel, Leipzig, 1851

in *Carmina*, vol. 3, ed. A. Riese, Leipzig, 1874

in *Carmina in exilio composita*, ed. O. Güthling, Leipzig, 1884

in *Poeti latini minori*, ed. G. Curcio, vol. 1, Acireale, 1902

in *Corpus poetarum latinorum*, vol. 1, ed. J. P. Postgate, ed. 2, London, 1903–5

in *Poetae latini minores*, vol. 2, fasc. 1, ed. F. Vollmer, Leipzig, 1911

in *Tristium libri quinque, Ibis, Ex Ponto libri quattuor, Halieutica, Fragmenta*, ed. S. G. Owen, Oxford, 1915

in *The Art of Love, and other poems*, ed. J. H. Mozley (with English tr.), London, 1929

in *Les Tristes—Les Pontiques— . . . Halieutiques avec. trad. nouvelle* . . ., ed. E. Ripert, Paris, ?1937

in *Halieutica* . . ., iterum ed. F. W. Lenz, Turin, 1956

Metamorphoses

   Die Metamorphosen . . ., erk. Haupt, Korn, Ehwald

   Band 1, 8te Aufl., Berlin, 1903

   Band 2, 3te Aufl., Berlin, 1898

Tristia

   Tristium liber secundus, ed. S. G. Owen, Oxford, 1924

OWEN, S. G., 'Notes on the . . . *Halieutica*' in *CQ* 8 (1914), p. 271 *et sq.*

PAPENDICK, A., *Die Fischnamen in griechisch-lateinischen Glossaren* (Diss.), Würzburg, 1926

PFEIFFER, (F.) W., *Quibus legibus 'non' et 'haud' particulae apud poetas Romanos positae sint* (Diss.), Marburg, 1908

PLATNAUER, M., *Latin Elegiac Verse* . . ., Cambridge, 1951

PLINIUS MAIOR, *Naturalis historiae* . . ., vol. 5, ed. C. Mayhoff, Leipzig, 1897

POHLENZ, M., *Die Stoa* . . ., 2 Bände, Göttingen, 1948–9

POLAK, N., *Primitiae Czernovicienses*, Czernowitz, 1909 [I have been unable to obtain this book]

RADCLIFFE, W., *Fishing from the earliest times*, 2nd ed., London, 1926

RADFORD, R. S., 'The Juvenile works of Ovid' in *TAPhA* 51 (1920), p. 146 *et sq.*

RAMORINO, F., *Raccolta di scritti in onore di Felice Ramorino*, Milan, ?1927

RAND, E. K., *The Earliest Book of Tours*, Cambridge (Mass.), 1934

RICHMOND, J. A., 'On imitation in Ovid's *Ibis* and in the *Halieutica* ascribed to him' in *Atti del Convegno Internazionale Ovidiano, Sulmona*, 1958 [vol. 2, p. 9 *et sq.*], Rome, 1959

────── and SKUTSCH, O., 'Restorations in the *Halieutica*' in *Ovidiana, recherches sur Ovide, publiées . . . par N. I. Herescu* [p. 445 *et sq.*], Paris, 1958

RIEMANN, O., *Syntaxe latine*, ed. 7, Paris, 1927

RIESE, A., 'Bericht über die Literatur zu Ovid' in *JAW* 14 (1878), p. 255 *et sq.*

ROHDE, A., *De Ovidi arte epica capita duo* (Diss.), Berlin, 1929

SAINT-DENIS, E. DE, *Le vocabulaire des animaux marins en latin classique*, Paris, 1947

'Ichtyologie et philologie?' in *REA* 47 (1945), p. 282 *et sq.*

'Quelques bévues de Pline l'Ancien dans ses livres des poissons' in *RPh* III 18 (1944), p. 153 *et sq.*

'Quelques noms de poissons en latine classique' in *LEC* 12 (1943), p. 129 *et sq.*

'Pour les "Halieutiques" d'Ovide' in *LEC* 25 (1957), p. 417 *et sq.*

SANDYS, J. E., *A Companion to Latin Studies*, ed. 3, Cambridge, 1921

SCHANZ, M. and HOSIUS, C., *Geschichte der römischen Literatur*, Band 2 (4te Aufl.), Munich, 1935

SCHENKL, H., 'Zur Kritik und Überlieferungsgeschichte des Grattius und anderer lateinischer Dichter' in *JKPh* Supplementband 24 (1898), p. 384 *et sq.*

SCHENKL, K., 'Zu den Halieutica des Ovidius' in *Ph* 22 (1865), p. 540 *et sq.*

SCHMID, G., 'Die Fische in Ovids Halieuticon . . .' in *Ph* Supplementband 11 (1909), p. 253 *et sq.*

SCHMIDT, AEMILIUS (Emil), *De poetico sermonis argenteae latinitatis colore* (Diss.), Breslau, 1909

SCHÖNWITZ, W., *De RE praepositionis usu et notione* (Diss.), Marburg, 1912

SCHUSTER, M., *Untersuchungen zu Plutarchs Dialog De Sollertia Animalium* (Diss.), Munich, 1917

SCHWYZER, E., *Griechische Grammatik*, 3 Bde. (Band 1, 2te Aufl.), Munich, 1950–53

SEDGWICK, W. B., *The Cena Trimalchionis of Petronius*, 2nd ed., Oxford, 1950

SKUTSCH, O., see: RICHMOND, J. A.

SOMMER, F., *Kritische Erläuterungen zur lateinischen Laut- und Formenlehre*, Heidelberg, 1914

STEFANI, E. L. DE, 'Per l'Epitome Aristotelis de Animalibus di Aristofane di Bizanzio' in *SIFC* 12 (1904) p. 422 *et sq.*

STEFFENS, F. *Lateinische Paläographie*, 2te Aufl., Trier, 1909

STERN R., *Gratii Falisci et Olympii Nemesiani carmina venatica . . .* [see p. xxi *et sq.*], Halle, 1832

STOLZ, F., SCHMALZ, J., LEUMANN, M., and HOFMANN, J., *Lateinische Grammatik*, 5te Aufl., Munich, 1928

STRÖMBERG, R., *Studien zur Etymologie und Bildung der griechischen Fischnamen*, Göteborg, 1943

TAPPE, G., *De Philonis libro qui inscribitur* Ἀλέξανδρος . . . (Diss.), Göttingen, 1912

THOMPSON, D'ARCY WENTWORTH, *A Glossary of Greek Fishes*, London, 1947

THOMPSON, E. M., *An Introduction to Greek and Latin Palaeography*, Oxford, 1912

TIDNER, E., *De particulis copulativis* . . . (Diss.), Uppsala, 1922

TRAUBE, L., review in *BPhW* 16 (1896), col. 1050

UHLMANN, G., *De Sex. Properti genere dicendi* (Diss.), Münster, 1909

VERGILIUS MARO, P., *Aeneis, Buch VI*, erkl. von E. Norden, 3te Aufl., Leipzig, 1926

VOLLMER, F., see also: OVIDIUS NASO, P., *Halieutica*
    'Coniectanea' in *RhM* 55 (1900), p. 528 *et sq.*

WELLMANN, M., 'Alexander von Myndos' in *Hermes* 26 (1891), p. 481 *et sq.*
    'Juba, eine Quelle des Aelian' in *Hermes* 27 (1892), p. 389 *et sq.*
    'Leonidas von Byzanz und Demostratos' in *Hermes* 30 (1895), p. 161 *et sq.*
    'Pamphilos' in *Hermes* 51 (1916), p. 1 *et sq.*

WERNSDORF, J. C., see: OVIDIUS NASO, P., *Halieutica*

WILKINSON, L. P., *Ovid recalled* [see p. 363], London, 1955

WINTER, T., *De ellipsi verbi esse apud* . . . *Ovidium* . . . (Diss.), Marburg, 1907

WISTRAND, E., *Nach innen oder nach aussen?* . . ., Göteborg, 1946

XENOCRATES, *De alimentis ex fluviatilibus* in J. L. Ideler's *Physici et medici graeci minores*, vol. 1, p. 121 *et sq.*, Berlin, 1841

YATES, J., *Textrinum antiquorum*, part 1, London, 1845

ZIELINSKI, T., 'Les derniers jours d'Ovide en Dobroudja' in *Rivista Clasica*, 11–12 (1939–40), pp. 11–12 [I have been unable to obtain this article]

ZINGERLE, A., *De Halieuticon fragmento Ovidio non abjudicando* (Prog.), Verona, 1865 [I have not been able to obtain this, but it is 'umgearbeit. in Klein. Philol. Abhdlg. II', p. 1–44, according to Engelmann]
    Ovidius und sein Verhältniss zu den Vorgängern und gleichzeitigen römischen Dichtern, 3 Hefte, Innsbruck, 1869–71
    Kleine philologische Abhandlungen, Heft 2, Innsbruck, 1877
    review in *ŽöG* 30 (1879), p. 178 *et sq.*

INDEX VERBORUM ET RERUM